OLD WIVES' TALES

OLD WIVES' TALES

THE LOWDOWN ON EVERYDAY MYTHS

Peter Engel
and Merrit Malloy

ST. MARTIN'S PRESS
NEW YORK

Production Editor: David Stanford Burr
Design: Sara Stemen

Library of Congress Cataloging-in-Publication Data

Engel, Peter H.
    Old wives' tales : the truth about everyday myths / Peter Engel and Merrit Malloy.
       p.   cm.
    "A Thomas Dunne book."
    ISBN 0-312-09889-8
    1. Folklore—United States.   2. American wit and humor. 3. United States—Social life and customs.   I. Malloy, Merrit. II. Title.
GR105.E54   1993
398'.0973—dc20

93-25931
CIP

First Edition: October 1993

10 9 8 7 6 5 4 3 2 1

TABLE OF CONTENTS

ACKNOWLEDGMENTS

The Book Partnership, Merrit Malloy, Peter Engel, and Marsha Rose, wish to acknowledge our staff and researchers for their invaluable help on this text. In particular,

Bob Westal, who provided editorial assistance as well as pinch-hitting on researching and compilation of the text. He showed heroism in preparing and editing the final draft, as well as being the writer of several of the "Tales."

Maria Alexander, who researched and compiled much of the text.

Ron Ellis, who provided editorial assistance.

O'Brian "Mac" Wiest, who did the initial medical research on the presentation of this book.

And Rosie Chavez, of our permanent staff, who maintains our offices and lifts our spirits.

. . . And a special thanks to the *Fur* people.

ACKNOWLEDGEMENTS

BEWARE OLD WIVES SELLING BAD MEDICINE!

....

Though we've certainly done our level best to be as accurate as is possible in researching medical data, as total amateurs in every field but writing, we feel it necessary to make sure our readers understand that this book is meant *purely* for entertainment and should *in no way* be mistaken for a book of serious medical information.

Before you even *start to think* about making use of any medical information offered herein, *always, always, ALWAYS* consult your physician. In fact, you might want to consult two or three.

We thank you, our lawyers thank you, and the old wives thank you.

INTRODUCTION

Old wives' tales: Are they *really* words of wisdom? Or are they just hype?

The words we heard at our mother's knee, the things we think we "know," usually with utter, absolute, unassailable conviction, are almost impossible to shake without a great deal of help.

There are many tales: hair growing thicker after you shave it, chicken soup curing the flu, wet feet and drafts causing colds, arthritis acting up, birds flying low and seagulls coming inland when a storm is brewing, wine getting better when it "breathes." False, all false . . .

No, not completely. Some of the least plausible turn out to be largely true. Go figure.

Why do we believe old wives' tales even when they are demonstrably wrong? Why are we so trusting? Well, it is hard to disbelieve a "known fact" passed down to us through *generations* of wise women. We are simply conditioned from a very early age to believe what our mothers and their mothers and a whole heritage of mothers since time began have always known. But we also believe old wives' tales because sometimes, often when we least expect it, they turn out to be at least partially correct.

Sometimes old wives' tales die a natural death in the face of overwhelming evidence. Once Alfred Kinsey discovered that almost everyone masturbates, the old tale that this is a pastime that makes you blind, saps your strength, or grows hair on your hands had to be reconsidered. But while masturbation should have become acceptable, there are still plenty of sports coaches who urge total abstinence the night before a big athletic contest (an exhortation to which Wilt Chamberlain was evidently not paying close attention).

Nevertheless, self-correction of established old wives' tales is rare. Isn't it time, therefore, that someone researched the best-known and most widely believed of these tales and told you the truth about them?

That's exactly what we have done: from all the many and various tales and traditions, we've tried to determine what is really true, false, or a little bit of both.

To find out which is which, let's take a closer look.

OLD WIVES' TALES

OYSTERS ARE AN APHRODISIAC

"I will not eat oysters. I want my food dead. Not sick, not wounded—dead." WOODY ALLEN

How did this unassuming sea creature that looks like a shell full of phlegm and tastes like a burst of sea water inspire such a passionate controversy? Nobody knows.

But the debate has been raging since Roman times, when no orgy menu was complete without oysters. In fact, Seneca even wrote "An Ode to an Oyster" in which he gushed: "All stomachs digest you, all stomachs bless you."

Whenever it began, Casanova continued the legend by eating fifty a night before embarking on his conquests, and Napoleon ate generous helpings of oysters as he conquered Europe. It was the eighteenth-century equivalent of "eating your Wheaties." It did make good nutritional sense; there were no multitab megavitamins in those days and oysters are loaded with nutrients. A half cup of raw oysters provides 750 percent of the recommended daily allowance of zinc, 12 percent of vitamin B_2, 8 percent of B_1, 5 percent of calcium, and 45 percent of iron.

The only other way to get that much zinc and iron would be to eat six cups of wheat germ or thirty-five prunes. If Casanova had tried that each night he would have been famous in another way. But does this bounty make oysters a romantic stimulant?

"No," says nutritionist Bonnie Liebman. "People who have a zinc deficiency may have impaired senses of taste and smell. But it's not necessarily true that getting more zinc heightens the senses. It's not that iron and zinc offer any special benefits, it's that those nutrients are sometimes lacking in the average American diet."

So how did the oyster become associated with making love? Maybe because the oyster is so reproductively prolific itself. The female will discharge up to one hundred million eggs in a single season, while a neighboring male, stimulated by rising water temperature, will emit a billion sperm. Oysters also get kinky, changing gender and after a year or two changing back. Seems they're not called bivalves for nothing!

Aphrodisiac or not, people are crazy for oysters. They are now being eaten to extinction. The annual oyster harvest can't keep up with the increasing demand. Also, pollution and overfishing have added to the shortage.

Muskrat Greene of Deale, Maryland, a local legend, expert oyster eater, philosopher, and boatyard worker, holds the world record for oyster consumption. On July 6, 1985, he ate twenty-four dozen in one minute and thirty-three seconds. When asked if this meal sent him on a wild, amorous escapade he reported that he "mostly felt full." Still the legend around oysters is so strong that the mild-mannered Muskrat reports, "Whenever I go out around here, they lock up the women."

So although we have no hard evidence to prove oysters are an aphrodisiac, we have come to suspect they are a factor in causing some human beings to exaggerate.

COWS LIE DOWN WHEN IT'S GOING TO RAIN
....

"Just where does weather fit into the actual scheme of things? Is it science? Is it philosophy, or is it just the subtle comedy of God?" SWIFTON ENGEL

In the Far East the cow is regarded as a sacred animal, which gives it an exalted place in the Hindu community. Indians believe that if a cow carries her tail upright it's an omen of rain and if she slaps it against a tree or fence, it portends bad weather.

Country people in Pennsylvania, Wales, and probably many other places, insist that when cows lie down in low pastures, rain is coming. No farmer expects rain when the cows are standing or resting on high ground. Says one Iowa farmer: "My cows are a helluva lot more reliable than Willard Scott."

There is much folklore around the forecast of rain: frogs croaking during the day, insects flying low, gulls coming inland, old injuries or arthritis acting up, spiders deserting their webs. In fact almost any unusual activity in animals is said to predict a coming storm. Apparently, many animals have built-in barometers. If humans had this, the Weather Channel would be a continuous never-ending version of *The Gong Show*.

There is no fully reliable research on how many of these animal myths are true. But what seems to be proven is that animals react to the weather for one of two reasons: either to protect themselves, as applies to seagulls getting away from the worst of storms; or in physical reaction to ambient conditions as applies to bears hibernating because it is too damn cold to do anything else. So back to the cows. Yes, they do tend to lie down more before it rains, especially before summer thunderstorms. But that seems to be because it's hot and humid out. The simple fact is, cows lie down—as do we all—because they're, so to speak, simply dog tired!

ORGASMS WEAKEN YOU

. . . .

"If I had as many love affairs as I've been given credit for, I'd be in a jar in the Harvard Medical School." FRANK SINATRA

This myth, which prompts athletic coaches to advise against sex before big games, and advises students to give up sex while they are cramming for finals, is erroneous. There's no evidence that regular moderate sex saps physical or mental strength or endurance.

Of course, sex *is* exercise. It may tire you like any other physical activity of the same intensity. And if you stay up all night having sex instead of sleeping, you'll be just as tired as if you didn't sleep for any other, less pleasurable reason.

Orgasm releases tension and therefore can be a powerful muscle relaxant, thus helping us get to sleep. Some studies say they are a fine prescription for easing mild pain and certainly they ease menstrual cramps, thus encouraging a more relaxed night's sleep.

Regular ejaculation avoids prostate congestion, a painful condition that mimics prostatitis. Having orgasms (don't laugh) can be an excellent aerobic activity. Blood pressure, heart, and breathing rate all get a thorough workout. The mental health benefits can be invaluable: profound emotional release, closer partner attachment, and an increase in mutual love, support, and well-being. Sex is actually recommended for some heart patients as a therapeutic exercise on the road to recovery.

So, no, moderate orgasms in moderation do not weaken us. They may, in fact, be the most fun we can have while exercising.

THE SEXUAL URGE DECREASES WITH AGE

"My mother always used to say: 'the older you get, the better you get—unless you're a banana.'" ROSE NYLUND, "THE GOLDEN GIRLS"

Legend has it that two bulls, one a young stud, the other a crafty old geezer, climbed a hill and came upon a meadow of beautiful grazing cows. The young bull got very excited and said anxiously, "Let's run down quick and get us one of those beauties." The old bull stopped him and said, "I say let's walk down and get them all."

The phrase "life begins at forty" began in the Roman era, when the priestesses of Vestal were freed from their vows of chastity at forty and could start making up for lost time.

We have good news for the Vestals: many people remain sexually active into their eighties, nineties, and beyond. Normal aging leads to many changes in sexuality, but not to an end of desire. Sometimes illness or psychological problems will affect the sex drive, but ends only at death, when even phone calls and junk mail tend to taper off.

Physical changes are inevitable, of course. In women, the most radical changes come with menopause. Ovulation stops, fertility ceases, and hormone levels change. This can bring on "hot flashes" and mood swings, now largely eliminatable with hormone replacement therapy. Eventually the surges stop and hormone levels fall, terminating the cycle of ovulation and menstruation that began at puberty. Also, the layer of fat beneath the skin thins, the breasts change in size and shape as lower estrogen levels fail to stimulate the glandular tissue of the breasts, and bones lose some of their strength. (Take that calcium, girls!)

Men don't experience menopause (physically, that is), and most remain fertile into old age. Yet men certainly experience physiological changes in their sexuality. For one thing, testosterone levels decline with age. This doesn't change sexual interest or performance but it may explain why certain illnesses (diabetes, for example) and some medications may cause impotence in men.

Either as a result of this hormonal change, or perhaps simply as a result of a general slowing of all body functions, men take longer to reach orgasm as they get older. For some that may seem a disadvantage; for others (especially men troubled in their youth by premature

4

ejaculation) it may seem the greatest of boons. Older men may also find that, once they have had an orgasm, it takes longer than it used to to achieve the next one. Finally, some older men may find that their erections are not as frequent, reliable, or, in some cases, as rigid as they used to be. In *The Hite Report*, Shere Hite interviewed many older people about their sexuality. The consensus was that, as long as their health allowed, sexual desire did not diminish with age. And that enjoyment of "the wild thing" (if anything) actually improved.

Growing older may indeed mean that, in some ways, we get better.

MUSIC MAKES PLANTS GROW BETTER
....

"The only reason I ever talk to my plants is that they can't answer back." SIMON FANSHAWE

D oth music charm the savage palm? Are plants merely masses of unaware matter, bereft of sense and sensibility? Or do plants react to the sonic world around them? Are they all budding music critics who shrink from Led Zeppelin or the Sex Pistols but will weave a viny embrace around a stereo playing Bach or Gershwin?

That idea gained most of its backing from a 1973 best-seller, *The Secret Life of Plants*, which argued that plants have feelings as complex and varied as most of us. Strange as it may seem, this idea of music-loving plants drove itself into the national consciousness, spawning a movie and a hit record album for Stevie Wonder. Throughout the seventies many were sure that talking to plants was good; playing any sort of melodious, non-percussive music was even better. But was there anything to it, or was this just another manifestation of a goofy era?

The idea's roots (sorry) go back to when Charles Darwin played his bassoon for one of his plants to see what would happen. The plant, like most of us, registered no particular response to bassoon-music. During the fifties, Dr. T. C. Singh of Madras, India, conducted numerous experiments in which he is supposed to have produced musically increased growth in a variety of plants.

Closer to home, Eugene Canby, an Ontario, Canada, farmer

claimed to have increased his wheat production by 66 percent after the field was treated to Bach's violin sonatas. Botanist George E. Smith took a distinctly American tack by playing Gershwin's "Rhapsody in Blue" for a corn and soybean field. Once again, Smith found that the products of the rhapsodized field were substantially heavier.

Later, Dorothy Retallack conducted an extensive series of highly controversial experiments at Temple Buell University in which plants seemed to cringe when played acid rock, but would actually move *toward* speakers playing a variety of music ranging from Bach to Louis Armstrong. She was able to repeat her experiments on national television, when Walter Cronkite's CBS Evening News program broadcast her "proof" that plants responded badly to rock and well to the stylings of sitar-virtuoso Ravi Shankar.

But others are not nearly so sure. A survey of Los Angeles–area nurseries revealed that about half (usually the larger, more prosperous ones) had little or no interest in the whole matter of music and plants. Other proprietors reporting a suspicion that "nice" music and talk does have some beneficial effect on their vegetative charges.

The strongest "pro-music" opinion of all was given voice by Shelby Basso of Sassafras Nursery and Farms (a small organization located in the new-age mecca of Topanga). Ms. Basso is fervent in her belief that, after switching from her son's rock music to a program of semi-classical works, her plants exhibited far superior horticultural performance. She observes that those who treat plants like "plant matter" (a popular phrase in the nursery business) get "materialistic" results and those who use a more spiritual approach get plants that seem far more beautiful.

Our view is that the music probably doesn't do much directly, but if it puts *you* in a good mood, you might spend a little extra time caring for your plants—which can only help. Of course, if it's Metallica and Megadeath that puts you in a good mood, then you might consider exploring the joys of compost.

VEGETARIANS ARE MORE PEACEFUL

"A vegetarian is a person who won't eat anything that can have children."
DAVID BRENNER

Our vegetarian friends will not eat anything with a face on it. And they insist that as a result, they are infinitely more peaceful than we carnivores. It is true that you rarely see a vegetarian stressed out and losing it at the salad bar. It's hard to feel aggressive chomping down jicama and bean sprouts, but how far should we take this? Every time we get angry, should our first line of defense be steamed zucchini? If someone had fed Rambo a Vege-Burger, would he have moved to Berkeley and joined a men's support group? And what about the "fat and happy" vs "lean and mean" tradition?

To balance the debate we quote carnivore Bill Cosby: "Did you ever see the customers in health food stores? They are pale, skinny people who look half dead. In a steak house you see robust, ruddy people. They're dying, of course, but they look terrific."

We got to the "meat" of the controversy by talking with Victor Forsythe of the Vegetarian Society. He told us that "scientifically, meat contains adrenaline. When animals are slaughtered, they become terrified as they smell the blood in the air from the other animals. This fear causes them to release a massive amount of adrenaline into their bodies." Adrenaline controls the "flight or fight" mechanism of the nervous system—and the Vegetarian Society believes that this contributes to a person's being short-tempered or violent. If you look at places like Texas, where beef is king and bar fights are the norm, this argument seems plausible. But wait. Millions of mild-mannered, upstanding citizens eat meat every day and do not "go ballistic."

The National Live Stock and Meat Board notes an increase in malnutrition in youngsters who have eliminated animal products from their diets. Naturally, this is a clearly biased point of view. But no more biased, we suspect, than the well-documented views of born and reborn vegetarians—many of whom (apart from the health aspects of their choice) will not eat meat simply out of their consideration and love for animals.

The late vege-radical Marty Feldman once said with simple eloquence: "I won't eat anything that has intelligent life, but I'd gladly eat a network executive or a politician."

7

HORSESHOES BRING YOU LUCK

"Never send a man to do a horse's job."   MR. ED

Sure they do. *Everybody* knows that.

Horseshoes were traditionally nailed on the thresholds of doors in London during the seventeenth century. A popular greeting of the period was "May this horseshoe never be pulled from your threshold."

Farmers nailed horseshoes over their stable doors to prevent evil spirits from riding their animals at night, rendering them useless the next day. (The eve of May Day, you remember, is the night witches ride animals, a practice called "hag riding.")

When the butter didn't churn, all the up-to-date dairymaids dropped a heated horseshoe in the brew to break the spell. In Ireland, the country folk just dispensed with formalities and nailed a horseshoe to the bottom of the churn. One tradition holds that a bewitched horse should be fed soup containing horseshoes, nails, and iron filings. (Death from bad soup apparently cured the bewitching.)

To get rid of whooping cough, German folklore suggests feeding a child from a wooden plate that has been branded with a horseshoe.

The traditional custom around horseshoes is to place them *up* to bring *in* luck or *down* to hold *off* evil.

The varied superstitions are great for revealing human fear, but c'mon, do horseshoes really work? Some people wave purple umbrellas to keep away elephants. If you say, "Hey, there are no elephants here," they say, "See, it's working!"

So get yourself a horseshoe for good luck—but just to be on the safe side, we suggest you marry rich, don't smoke, and get an education, too.

MARIJUANA LEADS TO STRONGER DRUGS

"Cocaine is God's way of telling you you have too much money."
ROBIN WILLIAMS

"It's just a little dope, man. It can't hurt you."

Many people believe that the biggest risk of smoking dope is ending up doing a public imitation of Cheech and Chong. Others are certain that the road to ruin starts with that first puff. So what's the real dope here? Is pot really so bad?

It's been in use for over two thousand years. Ancient Chinese, Indians, Middle Easterners, Greeks, and Romans used marijuana in religious ceremonies or as a medical treatment. Then about six hundred years ago, the bad press started when an Arab historian blamed marijuana for causing the decline of Egyptian society. Unchastened, the Spanish brought marijuana to the New World in 1545 to use in making rope. Hemp was grown for this purpose in early American settlements, including Jamestown, as early as 1611. George Washington even cultivated the plants at Mount Vernon, carefully noting the fact in his diary. Beginning in the 1840s marijuana was touted as an herbal cure and was sold by pharmaceutical firms. But by 1937 it was effectively outlawed by the Federal Marijuana Tax Act.

Well, if marijuana has been around that long, and if it leads to the usage of heavy drugs, the kind that kill parents and maim their unborn children, then why aren't we all addicted, or at least brain-damaged as a result of our parent's addiction? The fact is that, while nearly all heavy drug users have previously used pot (the fact which underpins this old wives' tale), so have most non-users of heavy drugs. Moreover, virtually all heavy drug users used to eat candy bars before they did drugs. Does that mean Snickers lead to drug addiction?

Users of hard drugs started smoking cigarettes and drinking alcohol at a young age as well, but these factors are not commonly noted. The beneficial effects of marijuana have also been suppressed. Doctors have fought hard to eliminate government red tape in their efforts to prescribe marijuana to cancer patients. Apparently smoking grass is very effective in eliminating nausea attendant to chemotherapy. As one comic suggests, "They're still nauseous but they just don't care!" Marijuana is also prescribed for glaucoma.

What about brain damage? In a recent study by the National Center for Toxicological Research marijuana-exposed monkeys were found to have no evidence of brain damage. Noted researcher Dr. Robert Bloch at the University of Iowa also refutes claims about the adverse effects of *moderate* marijuana use.

Across the board, most scientists agree that continuous, daily, abusive use of marijuana (as with any other mood/mind-altering substance) leads to some adverse effects. Fortunately, the use of marijuana is slowing down. Smoking dope is (finally) no longer considered "cool"—kids really seem to be saying "no" to drugs.

Even for those hardcore pothead sixties radicals (some now actually in their sixties) who still "do" weed, we found no real evidence that partaking of marijuana definitely leads one to violence or harder drugs—yet. C'mon, doesn't it follow that one leads to the other? Not always. Sometimes it does, sometimes it doesn't. Comic Marsha Rose says: "You wanna see drug-related violence—ban cigarettes in the United States."

We have personally interviewed and have come to know (and even marry) several people who once experimented with marijuana. Most of these people (now parents) are good, upstanding, healthy human beings. Although many did continue to drink alcohol heavily, most did not go on to harder drugs. Those who did are dead by now—or wish they were. Others reclaimed their lives in twelve-step programs.

On the other hand, we are not suggesting that marijuana is good for you. It has been linked to infertility, increased heart rate, panic attacks, and sensory distractions that contribute to anxiety, paranoia, and depression. Research claims that long-term use can lead to impaired hand/eye coordination [??]. And inhaling the stuff can't be good for lungs—maybe Bill Clinton was on the right track. As Arsenio Hall says: "If God wanted us high, he would've given us wings."

There is *no question* that misuse of drugs does great harm. In no way do we support *any use* of marijuana. Yet, in the midst of dispelling myths, we do refute the old wives irreversibly on this one and say categorically that *no*, smoking marijuana does not automatically lead one to hard drugs. However, the experience of having smoked marijuana does generally guarantee that one will go on to become a more annoying and vigilant parent.

CARROTS HELP YOU SEE IN THE DARK

"Large, naked, raw carrots are acceptable as food only to those who live in hutches eagerly awaiting Easter." FRAN LEBOWITZ

Yes, they do, but probably no better than Cheerios do. You see, carrots contain beta carotene, a natural source of vitamin A. So, if you have a low level of vitamin A, and especially if you plan to drive at night, eating carrots will help. The lower your level, the more the carrots will help you. But one ounce of Cheerios (and many other cereals) with milk gives you most of your daily vitamin A needs, too.

The pigment in the eye that is responsible for transforming light energy to the brain contains molecules of a substance called retinal. However, retinal can only be synthesized by the body in the presence of vitamin A. If insufficient vitamin A is present, you may well suffer from night blindness. Moreover, constant flashes of light (such as from on-coming headlights), and the need to recover quickly from them, both require retinal, thus using up more vitamin A.

And go easy on those carrots or you might get something called carotenosis. Carotene is the red or yellow hydrocarbon pigment that gives carrots their orange color. It is also in egg yolks, sweet potatoes, and some leafy vegetables. Too much carrot consumption will make the carotene build up in your bloodstream and your skin will take on a yellow pallor—a condition that superficially resembles jaundice.

What neither carrots nor any other source of vitamin A can do is to improve the night vision of someone who has no vitamin A deficiency in the first place. And in our modern world where so many foods—cereal, processed meats, bread, orange juice, etc.—are vitamin reinforced, that includes almost all of us.

HOT FOOD IS BAD FOR YOUR STOMACH

....

"To eat is human; to digest, divine." CHARLES T. COPELAND

With all due respect to the old wives, if you listen to them *too* much you might end up not having much fun. A life deprived of such delights as chile verde, red curry, or pepperoni pizza would be a lot less enjoyable—at least for those of us who live to eat as much as we eat to live. And some of us just can't get enough of hot food. In fact, the more painful it is, the more we like it. We're the culinary equivalent of the whips-and-chains set; pain, in limited doses, turns us on.

So are we doing damage to ourselves beyond a painful burning sensation on our tongues? Should we be joining support groups? Well, in a manner of speaking, the answers to both questions is an extremely mild "yes."

First of all, spicy food may be, in fact, mildly addictive. CSIRO, Australia's national research organization, holds that capsaicin, the "hot" element of the chili pepper, provides a "big boost" of intensity that can never be matched by the more ordinary flavor effects of sugar and salt. This "boost" in turn may cause the brain to release endorphins, the natural pain-killer that is the source of the "runners-high," and the (healthy) addiction to exercise. Now, as those of us who work out regularly know, as far as intensity goes, endorphins are far from heroin. In fact, they barely rival a glass of beer. But still, a drug is a drug . . . .

As regards the harmful effects of hot foods, according to the latest research, hot food can temporarily upset the stomach somewhat in the manner of aspirin. A study at Houston's Baylor College Veterans' hospital had several men eat spicy meals and then examined their stomachs using a technique called endoscopy in which a video camera was introduced into their stomachs looking for damage. The camera did find some minor bleeding as compared to the control group, who had been fed a bland meal. On the other hand, the damage was nowhere near as extensive as those men who had been fed a bland meal along with an aspirin.

In another experiment Tabasco sauce and finely chopped peppers were sprayed *directly* onto the lining of the stomach (eek!). Again some extremely minor blood loss ensued but was gone when follow-up studies were done a day or two later.

What does this all mean? Well, for those of with healthy stomachs, not much. There is no evidence of any long-term damage. Besides, when you're looking for a cheap high, a little chili-pepper endorphin rush seems pretty darn harmless.

BAKING SODA RELIEVES THE ITCHING
OF MOSQUITO BITES

"Nature, as we know her, is no saint."   RALPH WALDO EMERSON

Ow! Slap . . . scratch . . . scratch . . . scratch. It's one of the sounds of summer when swarms of pesky mosquitoes hover hungrily around our bare skin.

And as if the bite isn't bad enough, the itching can drive us nuts, So what can ease our summer suffering? Common old baking soda?

Yes. If you have nothing else, the experts say that baking soda *will* work. Dissolve one teaspoon in a glass of water. Dip a cloth into the solution and place on the bite for fifteen to twenty minutes.

But wait! Other treatments are also recommended, such as an oral antihistamine, an over-the-counter allergy or cold preparation, calamine lotion, ice packs, salt with water mixed to a paste and applied to the bite, and Epsom salts (dissolve one tablespoon in a quart of hot water, chill, and then apply). Doctors also recommend aspirin treatment to help control inflammation. As soon as possible after being bitten, moisten your skin and rub an aspirin tablet right over the bite. You won't get any headaches on your bite either.

Of course the best remedy is *prevention*. Use a repellent to avoid the bite in the first place. Some mosquito species are active late in the day and therefore you may want to have protection if you are going out—especially if you are going near lakes, ponds, marshy areas, or visiting with Swamp Thing.

13

TOUCHING A FROG CAUSES WARTS

"Our ability to delude ourselves may be an important survival tool."
JANE WAGNER

Where would fairy tales be if the princess kissed a frog and all she got was warts?

It's understandable that people believed that frogs cause warts because these amphibians appear to have warts all over. But frogs (and toads) don't transmit warts and would be very offended if they knew what humans were saying about them.

Warts actually are benign skin tumors that occur singly or in large packs on just about any part of the body. Each type of wart has its own name, but they are all strains of the same common virus. Experts reckon that about 75 percent of us will find ourselves be-warted at some time in our lives. After acne, warts rank second as the most common dermatological complaint and $125 million is spent each year on treatments.

So what should you do if you get a wart? First of all, stop worrying—most warts disappear without treatment after a while, almost always within about two years. If your warts are sticking around and you don't have the patience of a Zen master, you might want to call in the A-team—vitamin A–rich substances to be exact. Twenty-five thousand IU of natural vitamin A from fish oil or fish-liver oil is the suggested dose. Simply break open a capsule, squeeze some of the liquid on the wart, and rub it in twice daily.

Ah, but warts are temperamental. They respond differently to this treatment. Juvenile warts can be gone in a month—more likely two to three months. More established warts might take two to five months or longer.

Apart from vitamin A, several other folk cures are available including vitamin E oil, clove oil, garlic, aloe vera juice, chalk, raw potatoes, milkweed juice, the milky juice of the sow's thistle plant (easily found in the thistle section of your local supermarket), and, our favorite, unripe fig juice (found, naturally, in your grocer's unripe fig section). Another remedy is to soak lemon slices in apple cider with a little salt. Let stand two weeks and rub the lemon slices on the wart. The remainder makes a swell cocktail mix.

One other supposed cure we really like involves taping the inner side of a banana skin to a plantar wart. If you don't feel like a total idiot with a banana skin tied to your hand then you might tolerate it long enough to see if it works. At the very least it should make you forget all about the wart.

Hypnosis has been getting some good notices for eliminating these nasty skin growths. Two groups were tested and three months later half of the hypnotized group had lost 75 percent of their warts.* One more victory for the power of the human mind.

MASTURBATE AND YOU'LL GO BLIND

"If God had intended us not to masturbate, he would have made our arms shorter." GEORGE CARLIN

W e're sure Ray Charles and Stevie Wonder felt strangely safe when they first heard this one.

But seriously folks, this is one that we feel safe in branding as not only wrong but weird. Of course, when it comes to sex, weirdness is par for the course.

It started as a warning from parents in the last century to stop their male children from committing the "self-polluting act." Incipient insanity, epilepsy, weakened physique, shifty eyes, and hairy palms were a threatened consequences of what was referred to as "self-abuse."

Oddly, females appear to have been exempted from this horrifying warning. Evidently, young girls were considered too pure to even contemplate such a pastime. For boys, however, truly barbarous practices were used as punishment for masturbation ("for their own good," of course). Spikes were inserted under their foreskins so as to cause agony when they became erect at night. If a boy was caught in the act, his hands were bound together or his wrists were chained to a wall. Even at the opening of this century, one American doctor assured worried parents that he would gladly "circumcise without any anesthetic" any known masturbator.

....
*However, they couldn't remember their mother's maiden name.

15

You have to wonder what these people were so afraid of. As we now know, masturbation is not only a predictable and natural act but is practically mandatory for male teenagers.

YOU CAN HEAR THE SEA IN A SHELL

"I have a seashell collection—you may have seen it. I keep it on beaches all over the world." STEVEN WRIGHT

Most of us have held a conch shell to our ear and heard the waves of the ocean, right?

In fact, this is an ear myth, a hearing trick—an aural illusion. The shell is actually acting like a tiny echo chamber. Its wide mouth collects the low-level sounds in the vicinity and intensifies them within its narrow passages. Because the inner surfaces of the shell are hard and shiny, sound isn't absorbed—it remains trapped inside the shell, creating echoes as it bounces from surface to surface until all its energy is dissipated. These echoes, so reminiscent of the sea, are the source of the conch shell's seemingly magical ability, but they are not in fact derived from the sound of the sea.

There are two types of mollusk shells: pelecypods and gastropods. *Pelecypods* have two shells hitched together with a hinge at the opposite edge from the opening. Clams are a classic example: they have two slightly curved and sometimes almost flat shells, and upon holding them to your ear you will understand the expression "to clam up," because there are no passages in which the sound can echo.

The *gastropods* are popularly called *univalves*. These are one-valved mollusks with only one shell. The land snails, conchs, whelks, cowries, cones, volutes, and abalones are among the members of this class. In most cases, the univalve shell is formed around a center column called a columella. Each complete trip around the column is called a whorl. If you hold a univalve so you can look down at the point or apex, you can follow each whorl with your eyes. The opening at the bottom is the aperture or mouth. The rim of this mouth is called the lip. Clearly, the canal, the whorl, and lips of univalves form elements similar to various musical instruments (like the French horn), and are therefore an excellent echo chamber for the sound of air passing through.

So the disappointing fact is that, when you hold a whorled univalve to your ear, all you will hear is a distorted version of the sounds surrounding you. In Manhattan, that might be the sound of taxis, their drivers yelling imprecations. In Arizona, it would be the sound of the desert wind whistling through the tumbleweeds and cactus plants. Only if you were at the ocean front, would your shell let you hear the true sound of the sea.

IF YOU CROSS YOUR EYES THEY WILL STAY THAT WAY

. . . .

"I'm a little upset. I just found out I have to have this little procedure done. Nothing complicated, but they tell me it is going to improve my vision about seventy percent. But I'm a little nervous. I hate getting my bangs cut." ANITA WISE

Eyes may become tired or strained from being crossed, but they will never lock together permanently.

Authentic research (among nine of our friends' kids) indicates that *all* of them have experimented with crossing their eyes. In fact, we've never heard of a kid who hasn't. But, while eyes may become tired or strained from being crossed, they won't lock together permanently.

But what happens to the kid who is forever crossing his eyes? Can eye-tiredness lead to crossed eyes after all? You do see a lot of kids with that condition these days.

Well, no.

The eye has six muscles: the superior, inferior, medial, and lateral rectus, as well as the superior and inferior oblique muscles, which control the movement of the eye and connect the eyeball to various parts of the socket. None of these muscles have hooks or sticky substances. All are meant to be used as much as possible.

In fact, some doctors believe that exercising your eyes—and crossing them is as good an exercise as any—is good for the eye muscles and may reduce the risk of weakened eye muscles later. It may even reduce the risk of (gasp), the dreaded strabismus.

Well actually, crossed eyes are a form of strabismus (or strab as the cognoscenti are apt to call it), an eye disorder in which the eyes are unable to focus on the same point at the same time. The truly cross-eyed form only a portion of total strab-sufferers, who are pretty rare themselves; the illness affects only about 5 percent of the population. Strab usually becomes evident in the first few years of life, but even the healthiest eyes have difficulty focusing during the first few *weeks* of life.

Before you have a panic attack and rush Baby to an ophthalmologist—wait. If, however, after a reasonable period of time the eyes are still out of alignment, it's time to take your child to a qualified eye specialist. Early detection is important. Often the eye has just turned a little and can be easily treated.

Eye experts vary on treatment but generally no child should be rushed into surgery without exhausting all nonsurgical alternatives. A series of simple exercises may be sufficient. (Ah-hah. How about eye-crossing ten times a day?) And there is a new light stimulation method which often proves to be quite effective. Some children find that, after a year with corrective glasses, their eyes have adjusted themselves.

So the next time your kids try to scare you by crossing their eyes, just smile and yawn and cross your own. That'll show 'em who's boss!

TOO MUCH LOUD MUSIC AND YOU'LL GO DEAF!!

"I'll go what?"   TYPICAL SIXTEEN-YEAR-OLD

The teenager lies on the bed, awash in musical ecstasy. The parent rushes in, screaming, "Turn that racket down, you want to go deaf?!" This little scene has been with us since the advent of amplified music. So is this a real attempt to protect their child's hearing or just another venting of parental spleen?

Sadly for megadecibel music aficionados, the truth is that continual exposure to moderately loud noise is a major cause of hearing loss. It happens like this: Sounds collect in the outer ear and vibrate the eardrum. In the middle ear, the three smallest bones in our bodies amplify and transmit the vibrations via electrical impulses to the brain. An excess of sound overstimulates and injures the hair cells inside the inner ear, causing permanent damage. Degeneration is progressive.

One very famous person who can attest to sound damage on the ears is Pete Townshend, The Who's legendary songwriter and guitarist. Today, he suffers from tinnitus, a persistent ringing in the ears. Townshend has lots of company. Other musicians suffering severe hearing problems include seventies headbanger Ted Nugent. Therefore, it's no surprise that many of today's hard-rocking musicians wear earplugs in concert, and this wouldn't be such a bad idea for the fans, either. Although the plugs do tend to cut out the high end of the sound spectrum, the sound is still superloud.

If you think you have a hearing problem, get your physician to refer you to an audiologist. You may need a hearing aid—or perhaps a newfangled cochlear implant (a still-experimental procedure that is currently being performed at the House Ear Institute in Los Angeles). But for those whose hearing is still good, it boils down to this: if you know you are going to be exposed to excessive noise, either take some earplugs along or take your chances on being able to hear less and less.

SPANISH FLY MAKES PEOPLE FEEL SEXIER

"A hard man is good to find." MAE WEST

Spanish fly is one of the best-known reputed aphrodisiacs. Where would dirty jokes be without it? Folklore is full of tales in which Spanish fly drives people sexually crazy. It is fiction's solution of choice to male impotence and female "frigidity."

Spanish fly is also called cantharides or blistering fly. It is made from iridescent beetles, *Lytta vesicatoria*, which are found in southern France and Spain. The main chemical in Spanish fly, cantharides, is very strong and is said to stimulate the sex organs. However, physicians warn that Spanish fly is basically an extremely harsh irritant. The irritating effect can cause dilation of the blood vessels which in turn can lead to erections of the penis or congestion of the labia. Alternatively, the burning or itching sensation may provide some users with a sense of genital stimulation. But such an arousal technique, more akin to dousing the gonads in Ben-Gay than true attraction, is generally unpleasant and dangerous.

Cantharides is a poison. Once ingested, it works by drying up the delicate mucus lining of the urethra, causing scratchy discomfort. The dry urethral passage then becomes sore and inflamed and swells the sex organ. We suspect that this was not the arousal method that God had in mind for us. And worse, the inflammation can also irritate the bladder, causing a more frequent (and painful) "urge." In large doses the toxins cause stomach pain and kidney shock. Very high doses kill.*

This substance was used to induce bulls to mate (they must have had a lot of ugly cows in those days), and it worked every time. But in humans, even with a smaller dosage, although the resultant passage of semen down the urethra soothes the itchiness for a while, the overall harmful effects of Spanish fly are now well documented.

Dr. Stephen B. Shaw tells us that there is the equivalent of Spanish fly in Chinese medicine. The Mylaboris or Tellini fly is used as an anticancer and blood-activating herb. Since it is irritating to the skin it can be sexually stimulating because of that itchy, annoying quality that we associate at times with horniness. But, like Spanish fly, it's poisonous. So beware, please.

A large dose of Spanish fly or Chinese fly can be fatal. Don't try it!

. . . .
*There is a product labeled as "Spanish Fly" for sale at novelty stores and other disreputable establishments. If you look at all closely at the bottles, however, the words "spurious placebo" are clearly printed on them. Evidently the manufacturers are betting that the kind of people who would buy "Spanish Fly" think that "spurious placebo" is Latin for "works really well."

BLIND PEOPLE HAVE BETTER HEARING

"Poetry is what Milton saw when he went blind."   Don Marquis

This is a falsehood based on a correct misobservation. It reminds us of the researcher who wanted to find out where fleas' hearing organs are located. To this end, he taught a flea to jump on command. Then he careful removed one of the flea's many legs. At his command, it jumped, but not as high. He removed the second leg. A further reduction in the jump. Finally, he had all the legs amputated. "Jump!" he commanded. The flea didn't move. "There," he explained, "that proves my theory: fleas' ears are located on their legs." According to what we want to believe, we can always find somebody to tell us what we want to hear.

To get to the root of this debate, we spoke to Carmen Apelgran of the Braille Institute of Los Angeles. Ms. Apelgran compares it to the old theory that we only use 10 percent of our brain. If you are sighted, then you don't rely as heavily on your hearing. If a sighted person and a blind person took a hearing test, the result would be the same. But when one sense ceases to function, the others become enhanced.

According to a study done by Seymour Axelrod, Ph.D., the blind are much better at the task of "sound relocation" because they are much more practiced at it. That is to say that blind people, out of necessity, develop that acquired skill. They can't actually *hear* better, but they can listen better. The input from their ears is processed in a more "focused" way.

Another myth we were asked to debunk while we're at it is the attitude that blind people have mystic powers or a sixth sense. In the movies there is always a small hut at the far end of the village, with a blind person who dispenses magic and sage advice in equal measure.

Sorry to burst another bubble, but the blind, although they enjoy "heightened" senses, are not endowed with special powers. So, the next time a blind person approaches you on the street, don't imagine they are having a psychic vision. They are just travelers like us. The blind are, in the actual scheme of things, pretty much the same as you and me, except that they can't see with their eyes.

FLUORIDE PREVENTS CAVITIES

"Be true to your teeth and they'll never be false to you."   SOUPY SALES

Does fluoride really do the trick?

The answer, as with so many of the best old wives' tales, is an unequivocal "yes," "no," and "maybe." Here goes . . .

First, there is no doubt that the regular use of toothpaste containing fluoride dramatically reduces cavities. "Look ma, no cavities" is more than a cute TV slogan. That is why the American, the British, the Pan-American, the Venezuelan and many other dental organizations have endorsed the use of fluoride in toothpaste.

Their endorsement is the more impressive (both in respect of the dentists and of the toothpastes) when one realizes that they are endorsing a treatment which cuts into their members' livelihoods.

On the other hand, whether fluoride in drinking water helps reduce cavities is far from proven. The problem is that the fluoride in the toothpaste works so well that the added effect of the same stuff in the drinking water is hard to determine. The consensus is that it does help, a little, maybe . . . .

On the other hand, some researchers have found hints that fluoridation in water may have some negative side effects. And dentists as a group have tended to say that at best it is unnecessary, at worst it may have unwanted, long-term disadvantages. Nevertheless, the American Dental Association remains unabashed in their whole-hearted endorsement of water fluoridation—a position that the organization has maintained for over forty years.

So brush your teeth with a known brand of fluoride-containing toothpaste, vote "maybe" on that upcoming fluoride initiative, and get to spend your money on your kids' orthodontist instead of their dentist.

LITTLE DOGS BITE MORE FREQUENTLY THAN BIG DOGS

It's something of a cliché in mediocre comedies: the small dog yapping at the hero's heels, pulling at his trouser leg and finally nipping off a tiny piece of ankle (ouch).

Smaller dogs are often accused of being more "snappy" and temperamental; it seems logical that their size would make small dogs insecure enough to bite first and ask questions later. But what are the facts?

The facts are that, yes, little dogs *do* bite more than big ones. Fortunately, however, it is usually not a very serious matter when they do. Indeed, that is one main reason why they do bite more often: they have been permitted to; there is less reason to teach them *not* to bite. (With a Doberman, you really do have to get the point across early on; with a Chihuahua, who cares?)

Another reason is provided by the late Barbara "Walkies!" Woodhouse (of PBS and BBC fame). "A vice I've met with in quite a number of small dogs is that they bite any person who approaches too close to an owner. This is nearly always caused by the owner's hugging the dog to her chest." Try doing that with a Doberman!

Some small dogs react out of fear. "Toy" dogs are frequently overly pampered and spoiled because owners tend to carry them everywhere. As a result they become insecure and frightened of anything unfamiliar. This causes them to withdraw from everyone but their owners, and then express their fear through aggressiveness.

Okay, so some small dogs are more prone to biting. But when bigger dogs bite it's far more serious. In an analysis of the medical records of the emergency room at Pennsylvania's Milton S. Hershey Medical Center, it was found that German shepherds inflicted more bites than any other breed. Small dogs accounted for only a small percentage of the bites.

But then, again, would you go rushing off to the hospital lamenting bitterly that you had been mauled by a toy poodle or a Chihuahua with a one-inch mouth? Embarrassing enough to reach for a Band-Aid instead!

The final truth of all of this is that the trick is to treat your dog with kindness and affection and you'll probably find the dog treats people the same way. We've encountered many sweet-tempered dachshunds, poodles, German shepherds, Rottweilers, and even one friendly pit bull—although we were *especially* nice to that one.

RED WINE CAUSES HEADACHES

"That's your idea of a romantic dinner, Oscar? Red wine and fish sticks?"
FELIX, ''THE ODD COUPLE'' TELEVISION SERIES

Wine can go to your head! Literally—and cause headaches.

In one typical research study, nineteen people who reported that red wine brought on their headaches were asked to participate. Eleven were given a red wine–lemonade mixture. The others were given vodka with their lemonade. Of the eleven given the red wine and lemonade, all but two experienced a migraine attack. Yet of the eight who drank vodka and lemonade, *none* complained of headache symptoms. Researchers believe the link is tyramine, a substance that is found in red wine and causes blood vessels to contract.

We might add, however, that our own personal studies in this field suggest that if the vodka drinkers in this study had been encouraged to consume several glasses of this hooch—let's say, oh, a dozen—they wouldn't have felt so hot the next morning either.

FISH IS BRAIN FOOD

"It has been said that fish is good brain food. That's a fallacy. But brains are a good fish food." MEL BROOKS

Suppose you're cramming for exams and go to the doctor desperate for something, anything, to enhance your brain capacity. What if he wrote out a prescription for pulverized liver or eagle hearts? If you had lived in medieval Europe the sages would have recommended just such an appetizer. And that's only the beginning.

In all places and times, putative brain enhancers have abounded. Asian wise men a few centuries back who wanted to get even wiser partook of ginkgo tea. Meanwhile in Europe, that enlightened monarch Louis XIV encouraged his court to nibble gold leaf in order to enhance their mental abilities. More digestibly, the lowly lentil was held during biblical times to have similar properties. Jumping up to the present, we have the nutrient- and caffeine-laden "designer drinks," said to be high-octane brain food by the avant garde.

Yet the most persistent rumor through the ages has been that fish is bona fide brain food. Is there anything to this? How come all those fish sticks we were forced to eat as kids didn't turn us into Shakespeares and Einsteins? Well, thought on this matter tends to divide into two, er, schools.

Some maintain that fish is excellent brain food because of its high protein content. Protein is vital to neurons and if they didn't function, we'd not only be intensely stupid, we'd be dead.

Fine, but why fish? Protein comes from a plethora of sources, everything from beef, legumes (ask your local vegetarian for the best protein picks), grains—just about everything you consume has *some* protein. Is protein from Chicken of the Sea really any better than protein from an actual chicken? Right now, the best answer seems to be, "not really." Protein is protein is protein. Of course, fish is also very low in fat and rich in many other nutrients, but it won't help you get an "A." Sorry.

COFFEE CURES A HANGOVER

"Coffee should be black as Hell, strong as death, and sweet as love." TURKISH SAYING

Your tongue is stuck to the roof of your mouth and your eyes feel like they've been through a car wash. You know you had a wild evening the night before though you're having a hard time remembering it. So, you drag yourself into the kitchen to make some coffee. But is this the best way to beat a hangover and sober up?

The main remedy, everybody agrees, is to replace the nutrients and precious bodily fluids you lose after going ten rounds with Jack Daniel's. Soups will help replace salt and potassium, but don't forget plain old H_2O, still the best thing for reversing dehydration. Alcohol also depletes B-complex vitamins, so foods rich in them (such as whole-grain breads and cereals) or a vitamin supplement certainly can't hurt. The same goes for amino acids.

And, yes, coffee (or anything else loaded with caffeine) helps—but in moderation. As headache clinic director Dr. Seymour Diamond explains to us, "The coffee acts as a vasoconstrictor—something that reduces the swelling of blood vessels that causes headache." So, a couple of cups may help to relieve the morning malaise ... but don't overdo it. You don't want caffeine jitters along with the alcohol jitters.

CATS ARE SMARTER THAN DOGS

(To Dreyfus the dog): "You're glad to see me every minute of my life. I come home, you jump around and wag your tail. I go in the closet, I come out, you jump around and wag your tail. I turn my face away, I turn it back, you wag your tail. Either you love me or your short-term memory is shot." DR. HARRY WESTON, "EMPTY NEST"

Frankly, this is a moot question—it's like comparing apples to oranges. As Mary Bly says, "Dogs come when they are called; cats take a number and get back to you."

Who's smarter? It's a no-win debate. It's like trying to pick the prettiest baby—never a fair contest. Animal ethologists say that even separate breeds of dogs can't be compared; each was bred for a different purpose. Besides, the two species are smart in different ways.

Cats are more independent and standoffish. Cat owners take this very often for superior intelligence. Dogs are more social and people-oriented ("Please love me, please"). Dog owners take this as proof of a dog's being more loyal—a civilized trait indicating high intelligence. Cats are acrobats. Dogs can be highly trained, but does this evidence intelligence or the lack of it?

Only in development are cats and dogs even close to equal. Newborn cats open their eyes a little quicker than dogs but dogs eat solid foods sooner. Female cats toilet-train their young but (as we all know from experience) female dogs are not as thoughtful. Otherwise, puppies and kittens mature at about the same rate.

If you happen upon a test to measure pet intelligence, please let us know. Until then, we tend to side with Jeff Valdez, who muses: "Cats are smarter than dogs. You can't get eight cats to pull a sled through snow."

Jeff does have a point. Dogs can be much more useful than cats. As Garrison Keillor reminds us: "Cats are intended to teach us that not everything in nature has a purpose." Indeed, the native intelligence of cats may be so profound that we don't yet have the tools to measure it. In the end we may find that a cat's brain may be as infinite as a dog's heart.

IF YOUR NOSE ITCHES YOU'RE GOING TO HAVE A FIGHT

. . . .

"The nose knows." JIMMY DURANTE

If your nose itches you would think that it means you should scratch it. Not necessarily. The old wives ascribe significance to itching on every part of the body.

If your nose itches it means you're going to have a fight, or kiss a fool, or meet a fool and be injured by him. An itchy nose also can indicate the receipt of a letter, or a call from an unknown lover, depending on the culture. It's generally believed that you should make a wish when your nose itches. (We always wish it would stop itching.)

Now, let's get this straight. If your right ear itches, someone has said something nice about you. If it's your left, someone has said something not so nice about you. If your right eye itches, you're shortly going to laugh, if it's your left eye you're going to cry. If your upper lip itches, you'll be kissed by someone tall; if it's your lower, by someone short.

If your knee itches, you'll soon be kneeling in a strange church. If your foot itches, you'll soon be treading strange ground. If your elbow itches, you'll soon be sleeping with a strange bedfellow.

An itchy right palm indicates that money is coming, and an itchy left palm that money is slipping away. You can break the spell of the latter, however, by rubbing the offending left hand on wood. Also, an itchy right palm can mean a friend is coming, that you'll soon be shaking hands with a stranger, or that you'll be having company.

So, yes, an itchy nose may foretell a variety of events (e.g., if someone lifts you up three feet by your nose, there's definitely a good chance that there's going to be a fight).

CHOCOLATE CAUSES ACNE

"I've smoked cigarettes and I've had affairs with Christians. But I never ate a Baby Ruth or drank a Coca-Cola." BETTY ROLLIN

So there you are, face to face with a sexy, soul-satisfying piece of Sara Lee chocolate cake. What could it hurt, you rationalize. It's only one piece, I'm young, and life is short. The next morning you pay the piper with an extra pound or two and (you guessed it) a zit the size of one of the smaller Buicks and a face reminiscent of the young Manuel Noriega. But was it the cake?

First the good news. Once and for all, chocolate does not cause bad skin. Spread the news. Acne* is not caused by Hershey bars! In fact, *The Journal of the American Medical Association* concluded, "even large amounts of chocolate have not clinically exacerbated acne."

Okay then, what foods do cause blemishes?

Some dermatologists contend that foods high in iodine like fish, shellfish, and kelp can cause zitty eruptions. Yet one North Carolina study of more than a thousand high school students showed that the substance has no substantial effect upon blemishes.

So what determines whose skin is pristine and whose looks like a map of Eastern Europe? As with so many hardships, heredity and lifestyle are the culprits. According to James E. Fulton, founder of the Acne Research Center, "Acne . . . is an inherited defect of your pores. Working women are especially vulnerable. They're prone to lots of stress, plus they tend to wear makeup a lot." It seems oil-based makeups can be particularly nasty. They contain fatty acids (in other words grease) that are actually worse than the gunk our faces naturally produce.

The Joy of Beauty author Leslie Kenton has another angle on the problem. "Many people with acne are victims of one or another food allergy and when the elimination of waste via the alimentary canal is inadequate, often wastes are eliminated through the skin." To combat this, she recommends a diet that is at least 50 percent raw fruits and vegetables.

So we suggest you conduct your own test—abstain from whatever foods or habits you think may be at fault. Cut down on oil-based makeup (assuming you are a woman, an actor, or a transvestite) and slow down on stress. Also, some over-the-counter medications, especially those containing benzoyl peroxide, are effective as maintenance. Staying out of the sun is a good idea too, as is a thorough daily washing of the face.

If none of this helps, please don't fret—lie back, relax, and count

....
*Though they are often referred to interchangeably, acne and pimples are actually two different, if related, syndromes (which, to add to the confusion, can both simultaneously affect the same area of the skin).

Pimples are individual pustules which may have a variety of causes—a piece of dirt getting caught underneath the skin, for example. Acne, on the other hand, is an actual skin disease involving a pattern blemishing of the skin. Their relationship to diet is more or less equivalent.

your luck another way because as bad as it gets (and we speak from direct experience) we promise you—*this, too, shall pass!* As the Irish sage Bridget O'Donnell once noted: "Better a face with a rash of zits than having no face at all."

FLEAS GO AWAY IN THE WINTER

"To produce a mighty book, you must choose a mighty theme. No good and enduring volume can ever be written on the flea, though many there may be that have tried it." HERMAN MELVILLE, *MOBY DICK*

There are fewer fleas in the winter, but sadly they do not disappear. They just rest.

Mike Rust, the foremost authority on fleas at the University of California Riverside, told us more about fleas than even fleas know.

There are many different types of fleas and each type lives on a different host, sort of the way corporate attorneys stick to corporations or entertainment lawyers stick to celebrities (parasites are the same the world over). One of the most common is the cat flea. During the winter it's too cold for the cat fleas to have eggs and for the young to develop. But unfortunately many adult fleas live through this yearly inconvenience and breed like crazy when the warm weather arrives. In nine months, two fleas can generate 222 trillion descendants!

In the Arctic Circle, fleas have adapted very nicely to their hosts in spite of weather conditions. This particular species of flea now survives the most frigid winters and can go months without eating. Mr. Rust says we can reduce some of our flea infestation by using insect growth regulators (flea bombs), vacuuming and practicing good sanitation. Some say traditional insecticide dips for pets penetrate better than sprays or powders. These dips, however, can be toxic, so follow the instructions carefully (e.g., don't use a dog dip on cats—what's good for Spike can kill Marmalade).

There are roughly two thousand types of fleas and if you think they are a problem now, it used to be much worse. In Europe during the fourteenth century (and several surrounding ones), fleas were notorious for spreading the bubonic plague or Black Death from human to human. Today they can still transmit a mild kind of typhus to people that rarely endangers a life unlike the full-out typhus, which can be fatal if not treated. In Elizabethan England, most people (including the beauteous monarch herself) wore flea bags, small horsehair-filled pouches that attracted the fleas and could then be disposed of with most of their boarders.

GOATS WILL EAT ANYTHING
....

"Part of the secret of success in life is to eat anything you like and let the food fight it out inside." MARK TWAIN

We've all seen the cartoons. Goats eating paper plates, tin cans, hydrogen bombs, whatever, as if they were the most tempting young rosebud. It's such a common image that it almost has the ring of truth. Yet, could it be? Is any animal capable of properly digesting a paper cup, let alone a can (tin or aluminum)? If this extremely high-fiber diet is for real, aren't goats the answer to all of our waste disposal problems?

And then there are our own memories. It was sometime in the mid-sixties at a Los Angeles petting zoo, when one of us can clearly remember feeding a voracious young billy a paper cup. Was it reality or the exaggerated, cartoon-fueled perceptions of a four year old?

True or not, it's easy to see where this belief came from. Certainly, goats are nothing if not exceptionally voracious and indiscriminate consumers. Goats, like cows and sheep, are ruminants, which means they are double-stomached cud-chewers whose complicated digestive tracks allow them to get the nutritional maximum from foods which to us are best used as stuffing for scarecrows. But even so, goats are exceptionally well-rounded in their selection of cuisine.

Classified as "opportunistic feeders" in farm lingo, they enjoy dining on grass, hay, grain, and saplings (but not, as far as we know, full-grown trees).

This lack of culinary discrimination, so helpful to wild goats in the fight for survival, has frequently created environmental controversies in spots such as Washington State's Olympic National Park where ravenous goats are threatening the local topography to such a degree that park authorities are contemplating staging hunts of the animals in an attempt to control their population. Goats have even been used as a sort of natural defoliant.

But all of this begs the question, will goats eat such nonedibles as paper, tin cans, or airline food? To get an answer, we turned to veterinarian Dr. Bruce Schmucker of the Pennsylvania Bureau of Animal Industry. Dr. Schmucker confirms that, yes, farm goats are exceptionally unselective eaters who have difficulty passing up even a rose bush (ouch!). As far as *paper* (not tin or aluminum) refuse is concerned, a goat might nosh on it—if it tasted good.

Dr. Schmucker compares this behavior to that of a family dog. Your dog wouldn't eat a notebook (even if had homework in it), but it might eat a candy wrapper if enough chocolate flavoring were left. Similarly, the goat in the petting zoo may well have eaten the four-year-old's paper cup if there were some residual sweetness remaining from the soda pop. Still, in general, goats would much prefer leaves to paper plates.

If you were contemplating replacing your trash compactor with a billy or a nanny, forget it. On the other hand, if you really *hate* weeding your garden . . .

WALKING UNDER A LADDER BRINGS BAD LUCK

· ·

"We must believe in luck, for how else can we explain the success of those we don't like." JEAN COCTEAU

This belief started in the Middle Ages, when it was claimed that, to walk under a ladder propped up against a wall or building would bring misfortune and indicate an affinity with the Devil. Not that this belief came from out of nowhere. Uh-uh.

A leaning ladder formed a natural triangle, and as the triangle was a symbol of the Holy Trinity, walking through it showed a marked lack of respect.

Similar superstitions exist in many non-Christian countries as well, where passing under any of a number of overhead structures is said to lead to misfortune. In modern Japan, telegraph wires are feared and many believe that if they walk underneath them they will be possessed by devils. Well, "believe" may be too strong a word, but they do have an uneasy suspicion . . . .

And, as we know, superstition transcends time. Today, in a number of European countries it is believed to be bad luck to reach through the rungs of a ladder for anything—and some Danish people still claim that walking under a ladder is an omen that you will be hanged. Of course Denmark hasn't hanged anyone in years . . . . Magic thinking truly dies hard.

Take heart, superstitious ones, there are antidotes! Should you inadvertently walk under a ladder you can cross your fingers . . . and keep them crossed until you see a dog. You can also try spitting on your shoe and leaving the spittle to dry. The theory here is to gross out the Devil (historically a damn hard thing to do).

We found no evidence that walking under a ladder will bring you bad luck. Actually, we tried it several times with no ill-effects at all (unless you count the paint the idiot spilled down on us.) And certainly, this practice does not prove your affinity with the Devil. However, if you drive a car under a ladder you may be regarded as possessed by spirits of another kind.

TOMATO JUICE REMOVES SKUNK ODORS

"Nothing ever really goes away." Mr. Wizard

Yes! It's true. Tomato juice actually works. Actually (honest to God), it removes skunk. *Reader's Digest* (no less) tells us that if our pet gets nailed by a skunk, saturating the affected area with a little jus de tomato will *significantly lower* the pew-level. Chemistry buffs take note: tomato juice works because of its high acidity. Of course, it's messy and sticky and it's extremely, uh, red . . . leaving the neighbors to think that your pet has either gone "punk" or been horribly abused.

An alternative is to give your pet a douche. (Massengill worked great for us!) Before you scream in terror, we are discussing a strictly *external* vinegar bath. Vinegar is good for covering up skunk odor as it is, again, acidic. Try pouring it over your pet, rubbing it in and sponging its face. Use rubber gloves to protect yourself from the skunk odor, otherwise you'll soon be giving yourself a vinegar bath. Don't let the animal get wet again, because water will rinse out the vinegar and the smell will return. You'll need a fairly large amount of the stuff and you'll have to repeat the treatment at least once.

Also, if you go to your friendly neighborhood pet store (don't take the skunked animal or they won't be friendly much longer), you'll find at least two enzyme odor eaters on the market: Skunk-Off and Odor Mute. Both have their own odor but compared with skunk they smell like Chanel No. 5. They work by mixing with the spray to create a whole new smell that's not nearly as wretched. Another nonenzyme product is Skunk-Kleen. It purports to have no distinct smell of its own. But after what you've been through, how can you be sure?

If the smell gets on your clothes you needn't throw them away. Simply soak them for several hours in a solution of a half cup baking soda and one gallon water *before* washing.

BAD THINGS HAPPEN IN THREES

"Two is company. Three is fifty bucks." JOAN RIVERS

Let's see . . . the Three Little Pigs definitely had bad luck, the Three Stooges were accident prone, the Three Musketeers lost their muskets, and *The Three Amigos* died a horrible death at the box office . . . .

Yes, a trend seems to be appearing here.

There are many bizarre beliefs attached to the number three. For instance, gamblers walk around the gambling table (or their chairs) three times before beginning to play . . . and they usually end up visiting their ATM three times before stopping. In an actor's dressing room three light bulbs are never turned on at the same time. It is also believed that you should never light three cigarettes on the same match (or use three matches to light one cigarette). To do so is to risk pregnancy—hey, we only report the facts.

In Christianity, the number three is said to represent the Holy

Ghost, the third part of the Trinity. In the Celtic religion it represents the universe. This superstition may have started when it got around that Peter denied Christ three times. Not two times, mind you, but *three* times.

The irony here is that the number three also can represent *good* luck. A lot of folk remedies require that you perform the rituals three times. Also we give "Three Cheers" for someone who has done something good. And, of course, a hat trick in sports causes cheers galore.

So widespread is the belief that when two calamities occur a third is bound to follow, that many of us actively expect it. That, of course, often becomes a self-fulfilling prophesy: We become hesitant, insecure and nervous, just "asking for it" to happen. And it usually does.

So whether there is good luck or bad luck turns out to be all relative. Three men in a tub sounds pretty bad to us, but it probably depends on the size of the tub. The three blind mice certainly had no fun. And we all know that, "while two's company, three's a crowd." On the other hand, three coins in a fountain is considered very good luck. *Three Men and a Baby* seems like an odd romance but it worked as a movie, so who knows? And "baby makes three" is one of the happiest phrases we know.

A BLACK CAT CROSSING YOUR PATH IS BAD LUCK

. . . .

"The devil made me do it."   FLIP WILSON (AS GERALDINE)

This belief is not as simple as legend has led us to believe. The color black is often equated with evil. And cats, everybody knows, are the most mysterious of creatures.

In America, black cats have always been considered unlucky— mainly because of their association with witchcraft. They got a lot of bad press from the Church.

In other countries the black cat is considered good luck. This superstition dates back to the ancient Egyptians, who worshiped cats.

One of their most important goddesses was Bast—a female black cat. The ancient Egyptians also gave us the "nine lives" tale, inspired by the cat's fabled tenacity and resilience.

In England a black cat is also considered good luck. Charles I of England had one, and when it sickened and died he lamented, "My luck is gone." The next day he was arrested. So, it's not surprising that they were bought and sold for large sums of money.

It is also held that a black cat walking into your house will bring you good luck. The animal is said to have curative powers as well. Blood from its tail is purported to cure many minor illnesses if rubbed on the affected body part. In many primitive areas of the world the black cat has been used in special rituals. Cat lovers can relax, though; there is no evidence to indicate the black kittens were ever sacrificed to appease the gods.

So whether you believe they are good luck or bad luck it's a good idea to treat black cats (and all other cats) well—just to be on the safe side.

FEED A COLD AND STARVE A FEVER

"When you can't breathe through your nose, tomorrow seems strangely like the day before yesterday." E. B. WHITE

Feed a cold and starve a fever, or starve a cold and feed a fever? What do the experts say? Dr. Elson Haas advises: "The very fact that you have a cold in the first place may point to a diet that puts a strain on your body's metabolism." He advises eating fewer fatty foods, meat, and milk products, and more fresh fruit and vegetables. Personally, we defer to tradition and run to the deli for some chicken soup. It's now proven that chicken soup can help unclog your nasal passages. Some say it's like liquid mom—a comfort surely and perhaps even a quasi cure. That's the point, of course, there's not much you can do about a cold, so you might as well try to remain cheerful. For some of us, a good solid infusion of doughnuts will work wonders. Others will prefer a hot toddy, don't skimp on the rum . . . .

There are, of course, several types of food, in addition to chicken soup, which their supporters claim actually help. Foods containing vitamin C are widely recommended. Many doctors recommend you increase your liquid intake. Some holistic doctors recommend taking certain herbs such as goldenseal and Echinacea, which is said to cleanse the blood and strengthen the immune system. Or why not feed your cold some garlic? "Garlic is well known to have antibiotic effects," says Dr. Haas. "It can actually kill germs and clear up your cold symptoms more rapidly." Of course if you take too much you not only lose your cold—you can lose your friends. On a more fragrant note, licorice root tea, which soothes irritated throats and relieves coughs, is also recommended.

As for a fever, that is an entirely different matter. First of all, you should remember that it is not an illness in itself but a symptom of an illness. Fevers are one of the body's most important frontline defense mechanisms against infection. Thus, knowing that there's something awry with the old bod, it's probably a poor idea to over-load it with a stuffing of food. Anyhow, who feels like eating a lot when your skin hurts, your head throbs and you're probably nauseous.

When you are hot with a fever your body perspires and you cool down. But if you lose too much water—as you might with a high fever—your body turns off its sweat ducts to forestall further water loss. So, as with a cold, drink plenty of liquids, especially fruit and vegetable juices as they are high in vitamins and minerals. If you are too nauseated to drink you can suck on ice or frozen fruit juice.

One problem is that when we run high temperatures our bodies may need more calories to combat the invading organism, although we may well lose our appetite! This is another reason to be sure to drink lots of fluids. Fortunately, most of us have a reserve of calories to last through an illness. But if you do have an appetite, most experts say you should eat.

But others differ on this point. Some prefer juice fasting until the fever is reduced to nearly normal. Which, of course, only adds to the confusion.

So now what was it again? Feed the cold, starve the fever? Yes. Maybe. Well . . . No—we know, it's feed the cat and starve the beaver.

BLOWING INTO A PAPER BAG
CURES HICCUPS

....

"God forbid anything should be easy." HAWKEYE, ''M*A*S*H''

Hiccups are bad enough, but sometimes the treatment is worse. Friends pound mercilessly on our back; they jump screaming out of closets and scare the pants off us; sometimes they encourage us to hold our breath until we almost lose consciousness. And, of course, they urge us to blow into a brown paper bag. But (hic) often to no avail.

If any of these methods worked reliably, then they should have helped Charles Osborne, of Anthon, Iowa, who started hiccuping in 1922 and continued until 1987! That's 430 million hiccups.

There are literally thousands of "cures." Everybody swears by at least one.

One cure that would have gone down well with Mary Poppins is put forth by gastroenterologist Andre Dubois—a teaspoon of plain sugar, poured down on your throat. "The sugar is probably acting in the mouth to modify the nervous impulses that would otherwise tell the muscles in the diaphragm to contract spasmodically." In other words, you gag (briefly). Cures sometimes veer toward the ridiculous: "I cure my hiccups by filling a glass of water, bending over forward and drinking the water upside down," suggests Dr. Richard McCallum, of the University of Virginia. Steve Laddy of *Prevention* magazine recommends a whole *tablespoon* of sugar.

As medical science has it, these treatments either increase the amount of carbon dioxide in the bloodstream or stop the blips in the nervous system that create all the sputtering commotion. But do these remedies work? Doctors say it doesn't really matter because hiccups usually stop on their own after a few minutes.

Then there's always prevention. "When you're eating, just be quiet and eat," says Betty Shaver of New York's New Age Health Spa. "Then you won't get hiccups."

When children get hiccups, "I tickle them while they hold their breath, and they try real hard not to laugh," says daycare worker Ronnie Fern.

But what about the infamous blowing into a brown bag? Most

experts are convinced that this method doesn't work. Mail clerk Pay Leayman disagrees. "It's in the technique," Leayman argues. If you hold your breath as long as you can before you blow up the bag, and then someone pops the bag unexpectedly giving you a fright it works just fine.

So solutions abound but the hiccup controversy rages all about us, and hapless victims around the world echo the plaintive cry of Charlie Osborne: Hic, hic, hic, hic!

COFFEE STUNTS YOUR GROWTH

"If this is coffee, please bring me some tea; if this is tea, please bring me some coffee." ABRAHAM LINCOLN

No, we don't mean that if you take a sip of coffee you'll turn into a munchkin. The old wives were simply implying that you might not reach your full height if you took to coffee early.

Fortunately for those height-conscious youngsters enjoying their initial confrontations with the caffeine bean, there seems to be no hard evidence to show that coffee consumption stunts growth. But should Junior rush to find happiness with Mrs. Olson or Juan Valdez?

Coffee certainly doesn't stunt your *intellectual* growth. Voltaire was known to knock back as many as seventy-two demitasses in a day, and Beethoven was especially fond of his Vienna roast, but it was superprolific French novelist Honoré de Balzac who was the ultimate "coffee achiever." Balzac is actually thought to have died from his coffeeholism, downing some fifty thousand cups of especially strong brew before confronting his final episode of caffeine jitters.

So what exactly killed Balzac?

Caffeine, the "perky" ingredient in coffee, is present in many foods: Coca-Cola contains 36.8 mg. per eight-ounce bottle and Pepsi contains 24 mg. Good old ground roast coffee, however, remains the caffeine king at a whopping 85 mg. per cup. Instant coffee (blech!) has only a measly 65 mg., and decaf a microscopic 3 mg.

In any case, overconsumption of caffeine does create harmful side effects. Pregnant women have been cautioned to use caffeine only in moderation, if at all. It is also a diuretic, and can aggravate colds and bronchitis. Studies on osteoporosis show that a slight amount of calcium is lost in the urine if excess caffeine is consumed, and diabetics should be aware that the substance raises blood sugar levels. A recent study at Vanderbilt Medical School tested healthy people who did not drink coffee. When they drank two or three cups, their blood pressure rose an average of fourteen points. It follows that hypertension sufferers might well consider turning down that second cup—or even the first.

The depressing litany continues. One study or another has linked coffee with: benign breast discomfort, endometriosis, diverticulosis, increased cholesterol, headaches, heartburn, hyperventilation, incontinence (ick!), impotence (yikes!), insomnia, irritable bowel syndrome (ick!!), menstrual cramps, Raynaud's disease, and (our personal favorite) restless leg syndrome.

So whether or not your kids take to coffee early, they will probably grow to at least roughly the same height as you did. If, however, you're a health-conscious "coffee achiever" *you* might want to consider doing some of that achieving on decaf. Remember Balzac.

RED WINE NEEDS TO "BREATHE"

....

"Wine is bottled poetry."   ROBERT LOUIS STEVENSON

As those suave characters in the movies first taught us, the custom exists of opening wine before serving in order to "let it breathe." This practice dates back several centuries and was initially for red wine—not white or sparkling. In those times the Burgundy or Bordeaux from France were high in bitter-tasting tannin. The resulting undesirable strong flavor benefited from airing out. This was common practice among red wine–loving Englishmen.

We spoke to Alan Tenscher, the winemaker of the Schramsberg Vineyards, Napa Valley, who said that 95 to 99 percent of today's wines do not need to breathe. It seems modern wines are processed more cleanly. Still, older red wines that have a good deal of earthiness can perhaps benefit from a little breathing or even decanting, according to preference.

Decanting, by the way, is the pouring of wine into another container so all the liquid is allowed to be exposed and mixed with the oxygen. Then it is traditionally poured back into the bottle by means of a funnel.

So if you are wondering how long before dinner you should allow the wine to stand, don't worry. Unless it's a very old red wine it doesn't need to breathe, or be given CPR, or put in an oxygen tent....

A votre santé!

TOO MUCH TV IS BAD FOR KIDS' EYES

One man to another: "They will never really crack down on air pollution until it interferes with television reception."

FROM A CARTOON BY CAPELINI

Watching MTV, with its relentless parade of nanosecond-length images, can certainly be a strain on the eyes. However, the two main issues with television's assault on eyesight involve the light source and proximity to the TV screen.

It's important to have another light source on while your child watches TV. Looking at a television screen is similar to viewing a low-wattage light bulb. Imagine staring at a lit bulb in the dark for hours and you will understand what happens when you lie in bed with only the TV on and watch a late-night movie. If your kids are video addicts, encourage them to take a break every few hours. As with doing any close work or reading, it's a good idea to let the eyes rest and focus elsewhere for a time.

It's also important to sit at least five or six feet back from the tube. There's less eyestrain at that distance, and less risk of exposure to radiation.

However, unless your TV is really old, the likelihood of it's leaking significant radiation is small. But, as is the case with any relatively new technology (especially when radiation is a factor), no one knows the effects of long-term residual exposure.

As for your child's mental development, lots of experts say less is more. Some disturbing studies have shown that kids who watch more than three or four hours per day have reduced thinking ability. It's like hypnosis: TV addicts look—but don't perceive. It seems that children watching TV sometimes go into an alpha state, which normally occurs during sleep. Alphas are considered nonvisual brain waves; when the eyes are open and the brain is focused on something, they disappear. It is possible that kids may continue this zoned-out state when they are reading or studying, making learning a lot more difficult.

So for any number of reasons, it's better to be safe than sorry and limit your child's TV viewing. Experts recommend a limit of one hour per day (they must not have kids)—two hours if they only watch on the weekend. That does seem extreme, but it really is a good idea to cut down and maybe give them a book to read. Of course, that means we grown-ups are going to have to set an example. "Okay, kids— *two* hours a night—okay, two and a half ... all right, three during football season ... but that's it .... Why, because I said so, that's why!"

PEOPLE GET DEPRESSED DURING THE WINTER

....

"Psychiatry tells us that one out of every five people is completely disturbed. And the reason is that the other four are nuts." DAVE ASTOR

When the winter months arrive do you ever get that urge to hibernate? To hide away like a bear from your everyday problems? Does it seem an overwhelming burden to get through your daily chores? If so, you may be suffering from the "winter blues," or, as medical science calls it: seasonal affective disorder (SAD).

Over time, with the advent of electricity, central heating, and other temperature-altering technology, man has adapted very well to the seasons. Yet, come December, many of us still get depressed. Perhaps it makes sense, then, that those most affected are artistic types. Creative people, after all, are *supposed* to be more in tune with their environment. Less widely known is that we can also be adversely affected by the summer. Some people have severe depression or anxiety during the spring and summer months—usually due to the heat. It seems that everyone experiences the seasons in different ways. Some find autumn a rush of crimson and yellow foliage while other see it as the mournful beginning of winter. Some find winter bleak and barren while others rejoice in snoozing by the fire.

So why? It's all due to the pea-sized organ tucked underneath the brain: the pineal gland. Each night, like clockwork, the pineal gland releases a hormone called melatonin into the bloodstream in minute quantities and continues to do so until dawn. The secretion of this hormone signals the duration of darkness and serves as a seasonal cue to animals.

But don't despair. There is hope for the seasonally impaired through a new treatment called light therapy. Patients who suffer from winter depressions are given "light boxes"—metal boxes emitting full-spectrum fluorescent light, which mimics the color range of natural sunlight on a sunny day. They sit in front of these lights when the short winter days darken early. Within a week depression usually lifts.

Probably many of the more sensitive old wives went through this seasonal roller coaster themselves, prompting them to warn us about impending depression. The power of suggestion being what it is, many of us got what we prepared for. We guess it's no accident we refer to the past as the Dark Ages.

TO STAY HEALTHY, STAY REGULAR

"I tell kids they should throw away the cereal and eat the boxes ... At least they'd get some fiber." DR. RICHARD HOLSTEIN

Bran, more bran. It's become the answer to everything. The veritable secret of life.

Americans are more concerned with having enough fiber in our diet and being "regular" than with many other serious issues. It is a national obsession! We are inundated with ads for dozens of products, all warning that if we don't have regular bowel movements a bad end is certain, either from colon cancer or from our own toxic pollution.

But what *is* regular? The problem is that each person is different, says Marvin Schuster, M.D., chief of the Department of Digestive Disorders at Maryland's Francis Scott Key Medical Center. "Many Americans are subject to *perceived constipation*—they think they are constipated when they're not. In reality, the need varies greatly from individual to individual. For some three times a day may be considered normal, for others three times a week may suffice."

If you are *truly* constipated, first make sure you're getting enough fluids—between six and eight glasses a day. Then look into your diet. Yes, fiber is a central weapon in the fight for intestinal fitness. Dietitian Patricia Harper suggests "the fiber should be complex carbohydrates such as those in whole grains, fruits, and vegetables ... (cooked dried beans, prunes, figs, raisins, popcorn, oatmeal, pears, and nuts)." Increase your fiber intake slowly to avoid gas. Families and friends will appreciate your caution.

Exercise is great encouragement for the bowels—even taking a walk—especially for pregnant women.

Meanwhile, nutritional chiropractor Grady Deal recommends eschewing all oils that have been removed from their original sources. "It's not the oil per se, but eating it in its free state that causes constipation and many other digestive problems," says Deal. "They form a film in the stomach which makes it difficult to digest carbohydrates and proteins in the small intestine."

So, no, you won't become ill if you don't have a daily bowel movement. But there is one more route to regularity. According to Alison Crane, R.N., president of the American Association for Therapeutic Humor, "A good belly laugh can help with constipation in two ways. It has a massaging effect on the intestines, which helps to foster digestion, and it's a great reliever of stress." So once again laughter is the best medicine, but prune juice might be more dependable.

YOU CAN USE UP ALL OF YOUR SPERM

"People make a living donating to sperm banks. Last year I let five hundred dollars slip through my fingers." ROBERT SCHIMMEL

How do you know when it's gone? Is it like a bank account that says "overdrawn" or a video game where suddenly you see "Game Over"? It sounds farfetched but a lot of us actually fall for this old wives' tale.

Before the invention of the microscope, semen was thought to be an exhaustible substance that had to be preserved at all costs. In fact men in certain tribal cults even drank their own (ugh!) in hopes of recycling this "precious bodily fluid." (Gatorade might have been a better idea.) Practitioners of the tantra, on the other hand, trained their disciples not to ejaculate—either when alone or with a partner. Tantric sex is practiced up to the present day (though more often as a goal than as a reality).

Short-term abstinence doesn't impact sperm quality. A man's internal reproductive factory keeps busy manufacturing huge armies of sperm-troops to replenish depleted forces. A recent survey studied specimens of semen produced after 12 hours and again after 120 hours. The sperm count, shape, and motility were not altered by abstinence. However, a *very long period* without ejaculation does produce fewer, less active spermatozoa. Evidently, the sperm tend to get lazy waiting for something to happen and just sit around, watching sports highlights, drinking beer, and munching Fritos.

By age seventy sperm production does drop, yet one study found some sperm in the semen of 48 percent of men aged eighty to ninety. Sperm from older men are not as energetic as those from their youngers, however, and, there is a slight increase in chromasomal disorders that can result in birth defects. The level of risk isn't clear, as few men start families after they hit seventy—although some certainly think about it.

So relax, you sexual dynamos! You are in no danger of finding yourselves spermless when you finally decide to procreate. On the other hand, you sexual slugs (you know who you are) need to give your lazy sperm an occasional thorough workout.

To quote the old wives, "Use it or lose it." They (almost) always get the last laugh.

OPERA SINGERS NEED TO BE FAT

....

"It's time to go on a diet when the Prudential offers you group insurance." TOTIE FIELDS

Of course, we know the opera isn't over until you-know-who does you-know-what. But must that concluding aria come from the lips of a woman who is, well, the size of Cincinnati? Must our popular image of opera always be a three-hundred-pound matron amazon wearing a Viking helmet and phony blond ponytails singing something that sounds like "hooya-a-ho, ho, hooya-aho, hooya-ho"? (Our apologies to Wagner fans.)

To sing originally meant "to resound." So does an extra hundred pounds of weight aid resonance? Or is it a smoke screen put up by opera divas so they can pig out without guilt?

One vocal expert states, "It is surprising how little we know about the physiological mechanisms of voice production, and many claims about singing by singing teachers in this respect are sheer humbug. The only facts we know for certain are that the voice is produced by the vibration of the vocal cords, and the resonating sound is a mixed sound which is amplified by the resonators of the pharynx, mouth, nose, and chest. We have no idea what anatomical circumstances favor the development of a big voice, or what it is which gives some very soft voices special carrying power."

Singers themselves don't contradict this. In the autobiography of world heavyweight champion tenor Luciano Pavarotti, he devotes a whole chapter to his love of food but does not cite this as a necessity for his powerful voice. Indeed, at twenty-five he was slender and his voice was already attracting considerable attention. The great Maria Callas managed to slim down while her voice remained as enchanting as ever.

As Pavarotti mentions, there is tremendous energy and concentration and discipline required in operatic singing. So, there may be a tendency to release some of the tension with an extra helping of spumoni. And who's to blame them if they can get away with it?

Weight is not mandatory for resonance or for greatness. It's just that some operatic giants, like the opera itself, are bigger than life.

GARLIC CAN KEEP YOU SAFE FROM GERMS

"Garlic is the catsup of intellectuals." ANONYMOUS

Aside from being credited with myriad magical powers, garlic does have a long history as a healing herb used to cure a host of ills.

To engender good health, Europeans placed garlic in a newborn's cradle, together with salt and iron, for the period from birth to baptism. In Sicily, it was placed in the beds of women during childbirth, and making the sign of the cross with garlic was said to drive away various tumors. In Greece, the physician Galen (second century A.D.) believed garlic to be an antidote to poison.

Other traditions hold that garlic can prevent sunstroke and intestinal worms. It also has been credited with curing dropsy and relieving hysteria. (We always bring a clove or two to business meetings.) Early Americans believed it would cure a snakebite, though it was probably more a last meal than an antidote.

The list of uses for garlic through the ages is endless—some even believed that wearing garlic would ensure that you would never become ill. Garlic is still used widely as a preventative, especially by nutritionists and holistic medical practitioners, yet to the AMA's great relief people continue to get sick.

But does this litany of medical folklore have scientific validity?

In lab tests, garlic juice has been shown to inhibit many bacteria and fungi. Some studies showed that garlic helps reduce LDL (the "bad" cholesterol) in the blood and increase levels of HDL (the "good" cholesterol). Other studies show that large amounts of garlic enhance the process by which our bodies break up potentially dangerous blood clots. Garlic is also one of the best sources of selenium—which cancer researchers have cited for its impressive antioxidant properties. Other experts also claim antibiotic properties for garlic and prescribe it for colds and sinusitis. One doctor prescribes it for his diabetic female patients to prevent yeast infections.

Very impressive indeed for an old wives' tale.

But you say you don't want that odor following you around? You can try chewing on some parsley or using mouthwash every fifteen seconds. Or try commercially produced deodorized garlic capsules.

Be aware, however, that some experts think that the processing of such products may reduce garlic's effectiveness.

Hey, maybe the old wives' saying is true and "garlic is as good as ten mothers." We'll let you ponder just how scary that amount of good might be.

WHEN YOUR PLANE ASCENDS OR DESCENDS, SWALLOWING WILL UNCLOG YOUR EARS

"I flew to London on the Concorde. It goes faster than the speed of sound, which is fun. But it's a rip-off because you couldn't hear the movie until two hours after you got there." HOWIE MANDEL

Clogged ears on a plane flight are a function of pressure on the tympanic membrane, or eardrum. At sea level, the internal ear and middle ear balance against the external air and so the tympanic membrane vibrates in perfect harmony.

When you go up in altitude, the pressure decreases externally, and the ear doesn't have time to adjust. The membrane becomes concave and you get a sticking or barrel type of feeling. When you swallow, you force the membrane out and pop your eardrum. Yawning opens up the Eustachian tube, which is connected through the middle ear into the mouth.

Swallowing also allows the Eustachian tube to open and admit enough pressure to equalize the inside and outside pressures. This increases the pressure enough from the inside to pop the eardrum as well. (Of course now you may find to your dismay that you can hear the insurance salesman in the seat next to you.) During rapid changes in air pressure that occur as a plane descends, the Eustachian tube remains closed and it takes vigorous swallowing and/or yawning to even things out afterward.

The worst that can happen from a sudden decrease in outside pressure, especially if you have a weakness in the ear from infection, is that you could have sharp, stabbing pains or a rupture of the eardrum, and possibly bleeding from the ear in the most severe cases.

There is a technique called the Valsalva maneuver, after an Italian anatomist who recommended it for clearing pus out of an infected middle ear: cover your mouth and nose and blow out as hard as you can. The resulting cracking sound is air rushing into the tube. (Or it might be your head hitting the wall behind you if you blow too hard.)

The old wives were absolutely right this time, and we hope our explanation of it has been easy to swallow.

EATING RICH FOODS CAN GIVE YOU GOUT

"Eating and sleeping are a waste of time." GERALD FORD

Long ago this was heralded as the "disease of kings" because only royalty and the very rich enjoyed gourmet food and drinks. However, we now know that not all gout victims are eating high off the hog. In fact, just how much rich food contributes to the disease is questionable.

Gout is actually a form of arthritis—a buildup of uric acid in the joints—usually settling in the big toe. For some reason gout sufferers produce more uric acid than their bodies can handle, causing needle-like crystals to form around affected areas. It's not as bad as dropping an anvil on your toe, but it hurts like hell. Uric acid is a breakdown of substances called purines that are found in certain foods.* If you can eliminate foods containing purines, you should substantially reduce the problem. Unfortunately in gout sufferers, the body continues to overproduce uric acid on its own.

The largest proportion of gout sufferers are overweight men who are over thirty. So one way to reduce suffering is to lose some weight—but slowly. Fasting or intense dieting just raises levels of uric acid. Stress precipitates gout, so chill out. Alcohol interferes with the body's efforts to get rid of uric acid and encourages it to produce too much. So drink lots of water—it also helps prevent kidney stones from forming.

....
*Foods that are high in purines include: anchovies, brains, gravies, kidneys, liver, meat extracts, and sweetbreads. Less saturated are dry beans, peas and lentils, some meats, oatmeal, poultry, seafood, and spinach.

It isn't so much rich food that aggravates gout—it is *purine*-rich foods . . . and (forgive us the pun) you've got to be on your toes to avoid them.

HAIR GROWS FASTER AND THICKER AFTER YOU SHAVE OR CUT IT

··

"I'm bald and yet I have hair."   BOB NICKMAN

Sorry, folks, this is not true. Most people start shaving their beards, legs, etc., when they observe the first light fuzz. After they shave, the hair usually grows back darker and thicker. They conclude that shaving made the difference. After all, pruning a tree makes it grow back more vigorously, right?

The fact is that the hair would have grown in thicker even if left alone. Adult men's beards are heavier than teenagers' beards. Older women grow more leg hair than younger women. That is because they have grown from kids to adults, not because they started to shave. Old Orthodox Jews who have never shaved sport thick, strong beards; young Orthodox Jews, like other teenagers, begin with fuzz.

To prove a point about cutting hair having no influence on its growth, one of us shaved one of our forearms every day for six months. (The lengths we go to bring you verifiable information!) Then after a reasonable delay for the hair to grow back, there was (and there remains to this day) no difference between the two arms.

We also spoke to Kenneth Leslie Wilkinson, a stylist at the Michael John Salon in Beverly Hills, and he confirmed that cutting hair doesn't speed up hair growth, although blunt cutting of split ends often result in thicker-feeling hair. Hair grows at a rate of five to six inches a year—slightly faster in the summer. He believes this is because of a faster metabolic rate during summer.

Another old wives' tale to bite the dust is that pulling one gray hair will make two grow back. Again, not true. You will probably get more gray hairs as time goes by whether you pull them out or not.

Also some people believe that hair keeps growing after you are dead, but what actually happens is that the skull shrinks post mortem, pushing the hair out slightly. Fortunately, the dead are no longer concerned with grooming.

AN APPLE A DAY KEEPS THE DOCTOR AWAY

"A snack so good, people even eat the wrapper."
AD FOR APPLE GROWERS' ASSOCIATION

It's strange that the old wives decided to single out the apple, as it has historically received probably the most mixed press of any fruit. Of course it was this fateful fruit that Eve gave to Adam. But how did it redeem itself to the point that it became a necessary part of our day?

Ever since the Roman occupation of Europe, the tree has been given special status. A seventh-century English law states that a man who unlawfully cuts down an apple tree must pay a fine of a cow. (A cow and a duck if the fine is left unpaid for over sixty days.)

The apple has also signified immortality, eternal youth, and happiness. Arabs believed that the apple had curative powers, and in Scandinavian mythology, the gods kept themselves young by eating the golden apples of Idun, goddess of youth and springtime. In pre-Christian Wales, local beliefs held that, after death, kings and heroes lived in a paradise of apple trees called Avalon. Here in the United States, one legend holds that if the sun shines through the boughs of an apple tree on Christmas Day, the fruit will be abundant the next year.

But maybe the old wives knew more than they let on with this tale. Nutritionists have often been baffled by the choice of fruit, because the apple is relatively low in vitamins or minerals when compared, for example, with ultranutritious bananas or vitamin C–packed oranges. Then it was noticed that apples are extremely rich in soluble fiber and that this type of fiber is important in preventing a host of diseases. Aside from the well-known importance of fiber in keeping our colons happy, soluble fiber has an impressive ability to lower blood cholesterol levels and also helps prevent sharp swings in the blood sugar level (which is of special importance to diabetics and lunatics).

Also, apples contain a carbohydrate called pectin, which some studies have shown to further help lower cholesterol levels. Pectin has other benefits as well, including the fiberlike ability to promote normal bowel movement patterns.

And guess what? It may be that a daily apple can also keep you at a safe distance from the dentist. In a recent study, eating apples helped remove icky, plaque-fostering food residue from teeth.

So maybe history gave Eve a bum rap ... perhaps when she gave Adam the apple she only wanted to clean his teeth and lower his cholesterol!

CUCUMBERS REDUCE PUFFINESS AROUND THE EYES

"A cucumber should be well sliced, and dressed with pepper and vinegar, and then thrown out, as good for nothing." SAMUEL JOHNSON

The eyes have been called "the windows of the soul." But what if your windows are a little bloodshot or their lids look a trifle bloated? Are cucumbers the answer? Why not radishes? Or tomatoes? But wait! Before you throw a salad on your face, keep this in mind.

The skin around the eyes is not only the thinnest on the entire body, but lacks both sweat and oil glands and is thus exceedingly prone to drying and aging. The circular muscle surrounding the eye has no means of cross-support. So, if any part of it is weakened, the whole structure of the muscle is affected. A gesture like rubbing may stretch the muscle, causing sagging of the entire eye area. Then there's nasty old gravity.

Some mornings we waken with puffiness and eye bags, perhaps due to allergy, salt intake, or one heck of a bender. Also, if the skin is dealing with birth control pills, sinus problems, menstruation, etc., eyes can puff up to Droopy Dog/Marty Feldman proportions. All of these are symptoms of water retention.

To counteract this, skin experts agree that cucumber can help, though the reasons remain somewhat mysterious. Our friend the cuke, aside from making a great kosher dill, does have the ability to draw excess moisture away from the skin. (Raw potatoes will also do the trick.)

Additionally, the coolness of cucumbers may be of some benefit. Coolness is often the best way to reduce swelling. Here's the procedure: Take a slice of cuke (1/4 inch), cut it in half and place on the upper and lower lid. Lie down and rest for ten to fifteen minutes. Follow by cleansing your face as usual. Ah, you look better already!

For those of you who just can't believe that a mere vegetable can cure those small pillows, you can always buy commercial compresses available at many stores. Witch hazel is commonly used. But why spend the money? These products may work just fine, but they taste lousy, even with croutons and bacon bits.

OLIVE OIL PREVENTS STRETCH MARKS

"I have gained and lost the same ten pounds so many times my cellulite must have déjà vu." JANE WAGNER

Some skin professionals claim that stretch marks cannot be avoided—and certainly not by anything applied to the skin—while others swear by a host of creams, lotions, and vitamins. The choice is up to you. Oils do moisturize the skin and make it appear less stretched, but they don't really avoid the problem.

The main reason for stretch marks is a rapid and large weight gain. Skin is elastic and can normally stretch considerably to accommodate a change in weight. The tissue beneath the skin surface develops as we grow, but if rapid expansion takes place the tissue may be put under intolerable strain so that it tears and stretches the skin above. This shows as a stretch mark—a red line on the skin surface. In time the redness fades but the skin surface never reverts to its previous condition. Scar tissue will remain and the stretch marks look like pale, white, threadlike lines. This often happens during pregnancy, as well as during puberty, when changes in hormones sometimes cause girls to put on weight suddenly.

The crux of the conflict seems to be whether oils put on the skin will affect what is taking place in the tissues beneath. Unnecessary weight gain seems to be the main thing to avoid. Exercise and a carefully planned diet are important, according to *The Family Health Encyclopedia*. But of course those precautions don't solve the problem of stretch marks due to pregnancy.

There is much evidence to suggest that the unsightly marks occur more frequently in women who are deficient in zinc, vitamin B_6, or both. Both of these nutrients are necessary for healthy collagen tissue and for the maintenance of the elasticity of the skin. Women who are on the pill are particularly susceptible to deficiencies of these two nutrients, as oral contraceptives have an effect on the body's need for zinc, B_6, B_2, folic acid, and vitamin C. But then again, pregnancy should not be much of a problem under these circumstances. Once you do get pregnant, one beauty expert recommends taking these vitamins orally as well as treating your skin from the outside with vitamin E and either aroma therapy oil or cocoa butter twice a day. Nutritionist Adele Davis claimed that when one woman, who had developed stretch marks during her first pregnancy, took 600 IU of vitamin E and 300 milligrams of pantothenic acid daily during her second pregnancy, she found that the old stretch marks had disappeared completely and no new ones had formed. Several cosmetics makers recommend penetrating body creams to alleviate the problem.

But no one recommends olive oil. Maybe that was the handiest oil around for old wives in the old days. But vitamin E and vitamin supplements plus regular massage with a penetrating body lotion is the treatment of choice of today's new batch of old wives.

THE SIZE OF A MAN'S HAND INDICATES THE SIZE OF HIS PENIS

"One thing men can do better than women: read a map. Men read maps better 'cause only a male mind could conceive of one inch equaling one hundred miles." ROSEANNE BARR

The old wives are wrong on this one. Indeed, the connection between hand size and penis size is sheer phallacy. In fact, no other part of a man's body serves as a guide either. Of course, a tall man usually has larger feet than a short man, but this does not equate with any other body part. As any short fellow will gladly inform you, the man's "reproductive equipment" has a less constant relationship to body size than any other organ! How's that for cutting a myth down to size (so to speak)?

There is no correlation between penis size and sex drive either. Authorities agree that sexual energy comes from a complex interaction of a man's genetics, hormones, and upbringing, as well as body image, self-esteem, and general health.

Neither do possessors of enormous organs necessarily make better lovers. Pornography notwithstanding, there are men with very large penises who do not satisfy their partners. We shall not name names. But our beliefs today are more advanced than in the Dark Ages. In the 16th century Gabriele Fallopio (who first described the Fallopian tubes) advised parents of sons to "be zealous in infancy" in enlarging their child's organs. So some parents attached pebbles to their baby's foreskin. This barbaric practice still exists in some countries today where, in addition to causing needless pain, it carries a risk of infection. It also doesn't work. Though skin can be stretched to great lengths, the underlying structure remains unchanged.

So another tale bites the dust. Anyhow, if you want to find out the size of a man's organ you'll just have to do it the old-fashioned way—get him into a game of strip poker, and use a marked deck!

A FULL MOON MAKES PEOPLE CRAZY

. . . .

"Snap out of it." Cher to Nicolas Cage (after he has professed his love for her) in *Moonstruck*

The moon has always held a tremendous power over the human imagination. In cinema alone, full moons have been blamed for everything from sudden attacks of bizarre romance to what happens to perfectly nice wolf-guys like Lionel Talbot (Lon Chaney, Jr.) when the moon is full and the wolfsbane blooms.

One still common belief is that female monthly "cycles" are linked to the moon. Indeed, the word menstruation refers to an occurrence that takes place each and every lunar month. And we all know at least one horror story linked to PMS and how "some" women react at that time of the month. Add the effects of a full moon to cramps and swollen ankles and it's no wonder that females sometimes temporarily lose their sense of humor.

The connection between the moon and crazy behavior has been made in literature ranging from the Bible to eighteenth-century medical texts to editorials in *Newsweek*. And, of course, the word *lunacy* itself derives from the Latin word for moon, *luna*. In England, the Lunacy Act of 1842 actually defined a lunatic as a demented person who enjoyed lucidity during the first two moon phases and was afflicted following the full phase. Even now, many afflictions are popularly attributed to full moons, including psychosis, epilepsy, and suicide. Some physiologists have theorized that the gravitational pull of the moon actually influences human behavior. Since we humans are mostly water and the moon governs tides, perhaps there's some correlation.

There is, of course, a connection between the full moon and various forms of normal human behavior. Certainly, more billing and cooing, more mating and wooing, takes place when the moon is full and the air warm. Romance, its entanglements, and the moon are inextricably linked. But unless you think that a lot of that sort of behavior is a little nuts, we are disappointed to tell you that there is no scientific evidence that serves as proof positive that our behavior is any more erratic during a full moon.

Conversely, at least one study showed that the highest rate of admission to psychiatric institutions occurred during the *new* moon, not the full moon. A separate inquiry revealed that homicides also increased during a new moon (logical, since darkness is conducive to crime). In addition, an analysis of a Massachusetts emergency room logbook revealed that visits did not increase during the full moon, although one physician commented (probably under the influence of the old wives) that the patients did seem "loonier" than at other times.

Of course the same thing happens around tax return time. . . .

TREAT FROSTBITE WITH HEAT

....

"Hot is just like warm only louder." MARY (FIVE YEARS OLD)

What should you do if you have frostbite? Run to the nearest fire or jump in a hot bath?

Neither.

Frostbitten skin becomes cold, hard, and numb. When thawed the skin may appear blue or purple. It could swell and form blisters. The severity depends on the length of exposure to the elements.

The main priority, of course, is to get out of the cold or away from the harsh winds as soon as possible. If that's impossible, use your own body warmth to give heat to the frozen areas: tuck your hands under your arm pits and curl into a ball, like a hamster conserving body heat.

It is important to keep frostbite patients *warm*, but *not* exposed to high heat. It's not advised to use dry radiant heat such as a heat lamp or campfire. Frostbitten skin is extremely sensitive. Warm water thaws severe frostbite as fast as is safely possible (water conducts heat better than air)—104 to 108 degrees Fahrenheit is recommended. Do *not* boil or overheat the water.

Be careful when touching the skin so as not to inadvertently break the blisters. DO NOT give alcohol to frostbite sufferers! It can worsen the condition by causing heat loss. Warm drinks can be given if the victim is conscious.

Don't get the affected area wet with snow; heat loss is accelerated by moisture. And no smoking—it decreases the peripheral circulation, making the extremities more vulnerable. And—whatever you do—don't let the area thaw and then refreeze. The water crystals are bigger when the part refreezes, which causes more tissue damage.

So this time the old wives were right: warmth is the best treatment for frostbite, allowing the circulation of the affected area to return slowly, just keeping warm and allowing nature to do its business, in its own sweet, perfect time.

KEEP MAKING FACES AND YOUR FACE WILL STAY THAT WAY

"I never said I'd solve all the problems."
FORMER NEW YORK CITY MAYOR ED KOCH

Believe it or not, the old wives were partially right. Constantly making funny faces, furrowing your brow, or squinting will eventually create wrinkles and permanent creases in the skin. This may take decades of silliness, though, by which time age has added its own sweet touches.

To check out your own facial contortions, one expert suggests you look at yourself in the mirror as you are talking on the phone. To focus sensitivity, place a piece of cellophane tape over your forehead. This will make you more aware of when you raise your brows and how often. It may surprise you.

Pillows are another way faces get scrunched up. We press our faces into them all night, every night, and for about five minutes each morning our faces really do stay crinkled up. So, learn to sleep on your back or experiment with side positions. Excuse the pun but, let's face it, our skin can stand only so much pushing around.

To further encourage and protect our skin, we can stay out of the sun, upgrade our diets, cut down on alcohol (which puffs up the skin), exercise, and add minerals and vitamins (zinc, C, and A are especially good). Watch out for yo-yo dieting, too. Repeated gaining and losing of a lot of weight is hard on skin.

Finally a word from the Far East. Doctor of Oriental medicine Marshall Ho says that the Oriental way is "from the inside out." He teaches exercises to help the tone and symmetry of the face and neck as well as acupressure and acupuncture treatments. But what can the layperson do? "Massage your face in outgoing circles using your fingertips, your thumbs, and the palms of your hands." This can restore the symmetry of facial muscles lost through age and years of a rigid expression.

So this old wives' tale is true—in principle.

WRAP A DIRTY SOCK AROUND THE NECK TO CURE LARYNGITIS

....

"Most times the cure is worse than the disease."
ARCHIE BUNKER,
"ALL IN THE FAMILY"

The old wives soaked a sock in some warming diaphoretic herbs, like chamomile, peppermint, and cayenne pepper. Maybe some chrysanthemum, or some forsythia. So when they said "dirty," they may have meant dirty with *herbs*. They brewed up some herbs, soaked the sock, then wrapped it around the throat almost like a poultice. They may have placed some eucalyptus leaves on the throat as well.

Laryngitis can be caused by trauma and strain due to overusing the voice, or by bacteria that attack the vocal cords and can cause spasms.

Viral laryngitis is probably the most common cause of hoarseness, which may hang on after other symptoms of flu or upper respiratory infections have cleared. No singing or shouting with laryngitis! This encourages nodules to form on vocal cords. These smooth, paired lesions form at the junction of the anterior and posterior of the vocal cords. They are commonly referred to as "singer's nodules."

Getting a nodule is a clear signal to stop the music and keep quiet for a while. Sometimes a speech therapist is needed. Recalcitrant nodules may require surgery, but most laryngitis is cured by resting the voice, taking over-the-counter medicines, and using natural herbs, with or without a sock.

ALCOHOL CAUSES BRAIN DAMAGE

....

*"I envy people who drink. At least they know what to blame
everything on."* OSCAR LEVANT

Well, it certainly doesn't make you any smarter. In fact, alcohol causes many problems. First off, alcohol is a depressant. It slows down the central nervous system, which governs the breathing and heart rate. At extreme levels respiratory or cardiac arrest results. Most heavy drinkers lose consciousness before they drink this much. Yet a lot of people drink fast. John Bonham of Led Zeppelin died after ingesting the equivalent of forty shots of vodka. Boy, was he in a hurry.

Abused over long periods of time, alcohol affects the membranes surrounding the brain cells, interfering with the ability to transmit information. After a while the cell membranes harden, becoming resistant to alcohol. That's why many alcoholics can drink huge amounts and not appear drunk. Yet over time the brain cells die and certain functions are impaired. Most severely affected are those relating to visual and spatial abilities, short-term memory, abstract reasoning, and problem solving. The brains of some severe alcoholics actually gets smaller. Even hard-drinking teenagers showed a low-ered attention span as well as abstract reasoning and memory loss.

Drinking can sometimes bring on a condition called Korsakoff's syndrome, which is caused by long-term, excessive alcohol consumption and the resulting loss of thiamine. Korsakoff's victims often panic when looking in the mirror or reading a newspaper ... remaining stuck in the recent past, believing that "now" is the time period just before the memory loss occurred.

The underlying fact is that there is some truth to this old wives' tale. Beware! Constant partying is not only stupid, it turns out that it causes even more stupidity. As Anne Wilson Shaef points out, "Being unconscious is great for sleeping, but it's not too effective for living." Moderation, please.

A GLASS OF MILK BEFORE BEDTIME CAN MAKE YOU SLEEPY

"You give me powders, pills, baths, injections, and enemas—when all I need is love." WILLIAM HOLDEN (TO ANN SEARS), IN *BRIDGE ON THE RIVER KWAI*

According to a noted California researcher a glass of warm milk an hour before bed works, but so would bread or a piece of fruit. The thing is to avoid sweet junk-food snacks that can excite your system and then let it down; the same with heavy meals. Nobody disputes that milk provides tryptophan which is a useful natural sedative. But unfortunately milk's high protein content reduces the ability of tryptophan to get into the brain.

Also, if you are a little long in the tooth (say fifty-five plus) drinking milk or anything else before bedtime is not a good idea. The bladder is very insistent and insomnia can be a real problem. It ranks right up there behind the trusty common cold as the number two reason why people seek a doctor's help, Gallup polls say one third of us complain that we wake up in the middle of the night and can't get back to sleep. So drink as little as possible for an hour or so before you plan to go to bed.

The important thing is to watch out for worrying. Don't let yourself rehash a stressful day—think of something peaceful, or distract yourself with pure entertainment. Perhaps a nice cup of warm milk might help. But you'll do better with soft, soothing music or environmental sounds, or, best of all sweet gentle sex.

The old wives say the best sleeping pill is a glass of milk and a clear conscience. We say it's being so tired and content you don't even know you *have* a conscience.

CROSSING YOUR LEGS CREATES VARICOSE VEINS

....

"The Mary Hart leg cross is a technique, and it's not particularly comfortable.... Occasionally I get adventuresome and go so far as to cross the other leg, but it's been left over right for years!" MARY HART

This is a total myth. Varicose veins are mostly hereditary. Crossing your legs may mildly affect your circulation, but it doesn't create the problem, although both smoking and taking birth control pills may contribute.

A hundred years ago they yanked varicose veins out with hooks. Now saline injections, an infinitely kinder solution, are the most effective treatment.

How serious are varicose veins, and should you see a physician? The main complications concern clotting and rupturing. Clots are usually painful red lumps that don't shrink even when you put your feet up. Varicose veins at the ankle may rupture, which is dangerous because you can lose a lot of blood quickly. If this happens put pressure on the vein and get to a physician!

The good news is there's a lot that can be done for the relief of varicose veins. Strong, sensible flat shoes for women help, as do support hose. (They resist the blood's tendency to pool in the small blood vessels closest to the skin. Instead the blood is pushed into the larger, deeper veins where it is easily pumped back to the heart.) Laser surgery and the aforementioned injections are also helpful.

Yoga helps relieve varicose veins, as it aids in resisting the pull of gravity. Good deep breathing techniques combined with old-fashioned putting your feet up is also recommended. Get that blood back home to the heart.

Another good tip is to tilt your bed; even a few inches can help. Gravity works with you through the night. But don't do this if you have difficulty breathing or a history of heart trouble. And finally, keep moving. Go for a walk. Prolonged sitting, as your blood tends to pool, can eventually cause problems in your legs, crossed or not.

RATTLESNAKES RATTLE JUST BEFORE THEY STRIKE

....

"Snakes ... why does it always have to be snakes?" HARRISON FORD (AS INDIANA JONES) IN *RAIDERS OF THE LOST ARK*

We don't want to rattle you too much but, while you may get this warning, this ain't necessarily so. And when you're wrong about rattlesnakes—you may be dead wrong.

First of all, the rattle on a rattlesnake does not produce a rattling sound, but rather a buzzing sound. This sound frightens a variety of animals (including us) because they associate the buzzing with danger (and boy are they right). But the rattle is silent when the snake is hunting. The snake doesn't always rattle before striking. Often it rattles just because it wants to be left alone. And we believe in accommodating its every wish!

The tip of a newborn rattlesnake's tail has a blunt rounded segment, the prebutton, which is soundless. Usually, within a week, the tiny snake's skin is shed, and the prebutton is replaced by a bill-shaped segment—the *button*. This is the actual "rattle." Then, each time this portion of the skin is shed, a new, loose-fitting segment is added, thus, the rattle tends to become louder as the snake grows.

So, no. Rattlesnakes don't rattle just before they strike. They rattle when they damn well please; and that's when they strike, too.

Fortunately, not too many people have died after being bitten by a rattler. Indeed, unless they are seriously provoked, the snakes rarely bite humans. Nevertheless, we urge caution. If you hear a rattlesnake rattle or buzz, buzz off. You can't assume it will bite you. But then, again, you can't assume it won't.

SWALLOWS FLY LOW WHEN IT'S GOING TO RAIN AND HIGH WHEN IT ISN'T

. . . .

"It's an important and popular fact that things are not always as they seem." DOUGLAS ADAMS, *THE HITCHHIKERS' GUIDE TO THE GALAXY*

If it's true that swallows fly low when it's going to rain, why don't weathermen study swallows instead of meteorology?

Well, perhaps they should for there is a correlation, and it exists for two good reasons.

The first is that, in the fall, just before the inevitable onset of bad weather, the swallows migrate to better climes. Since the higher altitude winds tend to be against them, they tend to fly away at lower altitudes. Obviously, when they return in the spring—at the equally inevitable start of generally better weather—they tend to catch the following wind by flying higher.

Second, there is the fact that in damp, sultry, windless conditions, the sort that often occur before a summer thunderstorm, the insects emerge in happy, itchy swarms. But they tend to stay close to the ground (and close to us) so naturally that's where the swallows swoop to eat.

As for the meteorologists, well, they probably don't watch the swallows for the same reason they rarely open their windows: They're stuck in broadcast booths in front of satellite-generated pressure maps, quite unaffected by anything as old-fashioned and unscientific as the weather!

WAIT AN HOUR TO SWIM AFTER YOU EAT

"God cannot be everywhere and that's why he made mothers." JEWISH PROVERB

Good old Mom—she may have been wrong about a lot of things but this wasn't one of them. You really should wait before going in the water after eating to prevent a cramp or a "stitch," which could lead to drowning. This would be quite a severe penalty for not listening to your mom, kind of like being grounded . . . for eternity.

Stitches are the sudden sharp cramping pains that athletes, both professional and Sunday varieties, sometimes experience in the upper part of the abdomen. A form of muscle cramp, stitches are caused by the blood supply to the diaphragm being shut off by pressure from the lungs above and the abdomen below, like a bomb and a submarine attack at the same time.

So what does this have to do with food? Well, if you have food in your stomach you are likely to develop stomach cramps. Here's why: To aid digestion the heart pumps a large volume of blood to the stomach. During exercise, the heart pumps blood to the muscles, and the flow of the blood to the stomach is greatly diminished. Without the blood supply, the stomach muscles suffer from lack of oxygen and, like any muscle without oxygen, develop cramps.

Digestion and exercise compete for our body's assistance. Waiting until our stomach empties allows both activities to get their due.

Some sports medicine specialists suggest that we wait three to six hours before exercising vigorously, depending on our condition, emotional state, and what's been eaten. Also, intolerance to food like milk or wheat can cause cramps. So can eating too much, especially greasy stuff on hot days.

So, yes, waiting an hour after you eat before a swim *is* sound advice.

WATER FLOWS IN DIFFERENT DIRECTIONS IN THE NORTHERN AND SOUTHERN HEMISPHERES

There is a fascinating old wives' tale that water, when it spirals into a drain, flows in a clockwise direction in the Southern Hemisphere and in a counterclockwise direction in the Northern Hemisphere. It sounds suspiciously correct but it is not true.

The supposed cause of this is the Coriolis force, which has to do with the effect of the earth's rotation on moving objects. The Coriolis force explains why hurricanes rotate in a clockwise direction in the Southern Hemisphere and counterclockwise in the Northern Hemisphere. However, when you are talking about small events such as water draining out of your bathtub, the Coriolis force is so minimal as to be almost insignificant. It amounts to roughly three ten-millionths of the force of gravity. Bath water drains any way it pleases, no matter in what hemisphere you bathe. (Larger vats of water are another story.)

A while back, MIT researcher Ascher Shapiro did a test. He filled a huge circular tank (six feet six inches) in such a way that the water swirled in a clockwise direction. Shapiro then covered the tank with a plastic sheet, kept the temperature constant, and sat down to read comic books. After an hour or two, he noticed the water continuing to go down the drain clockwise (presumably because it still retained some clockwise motion from filling). But after *twenty-four* hours, the draining water reversed and spiraled *counter* clockwise, indicating that the motion from filling had subsided enough for the Coriolis force to take over.

Which leaves us to wonder what sort of people want to spend every waking moment wondering which way water spirals down a drain. But then we have our own share of plumbing problems.

YOU GET YOUR BEST SLEEP
BEFORE MIDNIGHT

● ●

"Sleep is like death without the long-term commitment." LEA KRINSKY

D oes that mean the rest of the night is wasted? Is there a best time
to sleep? Should I get to bed at 7:00 P.M.? And why?

The old wives were on the right track with this one, but they
lacked current scientific data. It turns out that what is important is
slow wave sleep, which we go into in the first portion of our sleep.
The slow wave or delta sleep alternates with rapid eye movement
(REM) sleep during which most dreams occur, and as our sleep goes
on REM episodes generally become longer and the restful slow wave
sleep phases diminish. It makes little difference when you start sleeping, the same pattern tends to apply. So, yes, you do get your best
sleep before midnight if you get to sleep early enough.

A common side effect of insufficient slow wave sleep is aches and
pains in the morning. You may become a chronic curmudgeon from
a lack of real restful sleep. Our bodies are like an electric car that
needs to be recharged during sleep. The main purpose of sleep is
the regeneration of nerve energy. And don't think you're passive
during sleep—you are *very busy*. There is repair of tissue, growing
or healing, restocking of organs and cells with fuel, replacement of
old cells. The heart pumps blood through the body, picks up wastes
and debris uneliminated from the previous day and takes them to
the areas of elimination. Only part of our brain is asleep as the
nervous system continues its ongoing processes while the body rests.

So, no—you don't necessarily get your best sleep before midnight.
You get your best sleep in deep delta sleep, which occurs more at
the start of your sleep, but continues intermittently throughout the
night.

CHEW YOUR FOOD TWENTY TIMES

"Finish your vegetables! There are children in Beverly Hills with eating disorders." JOHN CALLAHAN

We heard this parental refrain when we were kids. Some of us learned how to count this way—and also how to cheat. Remember the first time you didn't chew your food twenty times and nothing happened?

Did your parents have any basis for this bizarre rule? Maybe.

They may have been trying to help us stay slim. It's said that overweight kids eat faster than skinny kids. If you eat slowly then you become more aware of what you're eating and you enjoy it more. Another bonus is if we ate slowly we would feel full quicker. It takes twenty minutes for our brain to get the signal that hunger has been satisfied. Eating slowly does allow us to feel full on less food.

Digestion actually begins when your saliva's enzymes start to break down starches in your mouth. If we rush this process then the stomach is overworked, possibly causing discomfort.

So, yes, it's boring, but chewing your food twenty (or nineteen) times not only will help your food break down, it might help keep your weight down, too.

DRINKING MILK CURES ULCERS

"Don't be cow-dependent." BUMPER STICKER

When we think of ulcers we typically imagine an overworked executive, stressed out from the pressure of his job and worries that are literally "eating away" at him.

But ideas about how ulcers are formed are changing, and so are the treatments. The bland, milk-rich diet is a thing of the past, along with leeching and tying teeth to a doorknob. Science now knows that among the causes of ulcers are smoking, high-fat diets, and chronic use of aspirin. Many doctors fault stomach acid as well as certain bacteria. Stress is just one more added negative factor.

The most important treatment for ulcers seems to be common

sense, whether you have a gastric ulcer (in your stomach) or a duodenal (on the duodenum). If something makes your stomach burn after you eat it, don't eat it.

The biggest surprise is that milk is *not* suggested for ulcer sufferers. Now we know that although it buffers acid for a while, providing temporary relief, it actually stimulates the production of acid and causes more damage to the stomach. Coffee also increases stomach acid secretion and causes more trouble later on. Avoiding chili powder and black pepper may be wise as they promote stomach acid as well as burning twice. Many doctors advise against alcohol, as it also stimulates acid secretions. Another substance likely to aggravate ulcers is salt.

Medications like Tagamet (which regulates acid) are recommended for ulcer patients by prescription.* Some protection against ulcer formation may be in the linoleic acid in polyunsaturated vegetable oil. The oil seems to protect against the harsh effect of aspirin.

So beware of this old wives' tale. Not only is milk not a cure for ulcers, it may cause a lesion to become worse. Ease up on stress, take life a little less seriously, and enjoy yourself. As Bart Simpson puts it: "Don't have a cow, man!"

GALLBLADDER TROUBLES RUN IN FAMILIES
....

"There seems to be a cure for everything but heredity." FOLK SAYING

W hile there is ongoing research and debate about the exact causes of gallstones and gallbladder diseases, all experts agree that heredity is a factor. Gallbladder trouble clearly runs in families.

Another risk factor is infection, which triggers gallbladder problems as well as bile composition. (The gallbladder's function is to store bile, a substance used in the digestive process.)

It has long been widely known that certain people are more susceptible to gallstones—overweight women, American Indians from the southwestern United States, diabetics, patients with inflammation of the intestinal tract, and the elderly.

....
*If you're eating antacids like candy and they're not helping, see your doctor.

Diet plays a role. The Hanes Study, the federal government's first health and nutrition survey, found that Native Americans consume a large amount of sugar. Fat and excess calories are also well-known contributing factors. The gallbladder is partially responsible for breaking down fats. When it's overburdened, it can't function properly. Extra calories and weight place a strain on all the organs.

The good news is that there are steps you can take to help prevent this problem from occurring.

If you have gallbladder problems, you need to consult your physician for the best treatment. Your doctor may recommend that you lose weight. Medication is another option. New drug therapies are extremely effective in reducing the stones. Surgery sounds drastic but some doctors actually favor it as a preventative approach. New laser surgery techniques have mostly eliminated the need for major abdominal surgery. Diabetics who have symptomless gallstones are good candidates for this to prevent silent gallstones from creating unexpected havoc in the future.

The main thing to avoid is fat. Even if you inherited a wimpy, problem-prone gallbladder, as long as you take care not to make trouble for it, it probably won't make much trouble for you.

FOUR-LEAF CLOVERS ARE GOOD LUCK

> *"You can take it as understood,*
> *That your luck only changes*
> *if it's good."* OGDEN NASH

The Irish are extremely proud of this tradition and they fanatically insist that it's "true as God himself." Actually, four-leaf clovers are not as rare as we might think. Many people wandering across summer fields find at least one. And these days many nurseries make a lot of money breeding them in captivity (which is pretty good luck in itself, we suppose).

In Great Britain folklore tells us that a young man or woman who finds a four-leaf clover will meet their future love the very same day. And you can double your luck by handing the four-leaf clover to someone else, passing the luck around. Another legend says that Eve took a four-leaf clover with her when she was expelled from Paradise, just to remind herself how wonderful Eden really was. One of the many clover-inspired sayings is:

> One leaf for fame,
> One leaf for wealth,
> One leaf for a faithful lover,
> And one leaf to bring glorious health
> All are in the four-leaf clover.

The phrase "in the clover" originated from cattle's pleasurable grazing in a clover field. There's also a tradition around finding a *five*-leaf clover (these *are* extremely rare), which ensures that you will become wealthy.

The shamrock (actually Dutch clover) and its adoption as the emblem of Ireland are due to the holy presence of St. Patrick. When first arriving in Ireland, St. Patrick found its people deeply confused over the Holy Trinity. He preached and argued but still they couldn't understand, until he looked to the ground one lovely day and found the divided triple leaf of a shamrock. It illustrated his point exactly. It was one leaf and yet three leaves in one. After the Irish accepted Christianity they treated the shamrock as their symbol of fortune— the three leaves representing love, heroism, and wit. Add a fourth leaf and you're "in the clover."

As the Irish tell us, dreaming of clover is fortunate, but finding one for real is true magic. And as we all know, the Irish never lie.

CRANBERRY JUICE IS GOOD FOR YOUR KIDNEYS

. . . .

"Cranberries are blueberries with an attitude." BRIDGET O'DONNELL

Rodale's *Encyclopedia of Natural Home Remedies* features several grateful letters from people who have treated long-term bladder infections with cranberry juice, like this rapturous missive: "It is a year since I started eating crushed up cranberries, a year since I

71

last took any medication for bladder infection, and a year since I've been free from it. This is after 40 years of this scourge!"

People with certain urinary tract infections are often advised to drink plenty of cranberry juice. Nurses give incontinent patients cranberry juice because it results in urine with less odor. Those recommendations obviously lead to the generally accepted "truth" that the stuff is good for the urinary tract, bladder, and kidneys.

The reports do differ. Some say the value of cranberry juice is limited to those conditions in which a reduction in the pH of the urine (i.e., making it more acidic) is desirable. Even then, cranberry juice is no better than any other acidic juice you might choose (such as orange juice).

Yet others swear by it. One doctor says it has quinolic acid (which converts to hippuric acid in the liver) and is fortified with vitamin C. Both hippuric acid and vitamin C have been shown to combat infection. The problem is, you'd have to drink gallons every day to duplicate the effect of antibiotics.

So it seems the mighty cran could have some healing potential. But not much. At least, however, as far as we could find, it can't hurt.

ACTORS ARE SUPERSTITIOUS

"Never let them see you sweat." ACTOR'S AXIOM

Theater people are legendary for being superstitious. We suspect that many old wives were performers.

Some well-known adages are: no whistling in the theater before a performance; it's unlucky to have pictures taken before the curtain rises; and never look over the shoulder of a performer while he or she is making up in front of a mirror. The lucky rabbit's foot charm is used to bring good fortune, and serves the added purpose of applying rouge. It is invariably kept in the makeup boxes, which actors insist should be left untidy. To knock one of these boxes over is a bad omen. Wigs are considered harbingers of good luck, and many actors will wear them when there is really no need.

Also, don't kick off a pair of shoes; if both shoes fall on their soles and remain upright then it is a sign of good luck, but if they fall over, misfortune will follow. And no actor would court disaster by putting his shoes on a chair in the dressing room. Actors believe they should always leave their dressing rooms with their left foot going out first. Should an actor's shoes squeak as he makes his first entrance on the stage, all will go well with the production. To stumble onstage will result in missing a cue some time during the evening, while catching part of a costume on a piece of scenery also makes for fluffed lines. The only way to undo this curse is for the actor to retrace his steps and make a new entrance.

In contrast, though, if a player spontaneously falls during a performance, he can be sure of another engagement at the same theater. A rule for costumers: peacock's feathers should never be worn, as they will bring disaster—indeed if these feathers appear anywhere in the theater, even in the audience, it is an ill omen. (Even a picture of a peacock onstage gets thespians unglued.)

Actors are indeed a strong breed. They're superstitious as can be. But then they wish each other well by saying "break a leg"!

THERE ARE NO BAD DOGS, ONLY BAD OWNERS

"When a man's best friend is his dog, that dog has a problem." EDWARD ABBEY

Are there bad dogs? Are the stories around the Doberman and the pit bull reflections of media scares, the animals' genetics, or their owners?

According to the legendary Barbara Woodhouse, "Dogs aren't born knowing what or what not to do; they only learn like children." Until we paper-train, discipline, give them the old sneaker to munch on, and put clocks in the beds, puppies follow nature's instincts. What we humans consider "bad" behavior in a domestic dog may be perfectly natural to his cousins in the wild. This includes begging for food, biting and chewing, and relieving their bladders at will any damn place they choose.

It's our job to retrain this instinct, to rewrite nature and call it "good behavior." Some negative traits or behaviors are due to physical ailments such as bladder infections or diarrhea. Irritating, moody behavior in an otherwise sweet-natured dog is a red flag that the animal may be sick. Never punish a dog for vomiting and other offensive but virtually involuntary acts.

Some people believe that you need to hit a dog to control him. This is *not true*. To teach, it is more effective to get an animal's attention by rattling pennies in an empty soft drink container or scrunching up some newspaper.

Dogs are so loving, so trusting, and so willing to learn that they would welcome a better-trained owner in the house. A dog would never subject any human to the abuse some of them have been subjected to over the centuries. Most people understand that they're not the dog's "owner"—they are just guardians, the dog's very human companion. Look around! These enlightened folks have the best-behaved, friendliest dogs.

But still, there are some dogs, as there are many humans, who have a tendency to be bad-tempered. "Designer dogs" from puppy farms with too much in-breeding may be genetically weak and chronically surly. Certain small dogs (as we have mentioned before) tend to be scared and snappy. Conversely, some breeds—beagles, Labradors, English sheepdogs, and Irish setters, to name just four of our favorites—are extraordinarily friendly even by canine standards.

So, yes, there are some bad dogs around. But most of them are trained to be that way. Very few dogs start out bad.

VINEGAR CURES ATHLETE'S FOOT

....

"There's a fungus amung us."   BULLWINKLE MOOSE

Folk remedies abound for that irritating itch, athlete's foot. The most popular is vinegar.

Athlete's foot is caused by an organism that lives on the skin and breeds best under warm, moist conditions. Moist footwear (e.g., sweaty sneakers) is a breeding ground for this pest, and it can take four weeks or more to cure the resulting itch.

The vinegar cure involves keeping the area daubed with the foul-smelling stuff all the time; clean stockings and socks can be dipped in a solution of water and vinegar. Or you could use wine. The folk recipe is: one ounce of sage, one of agrimony (an herb), and two cups of wine. Simmer twenty minutes. Cool and soak the affected area repeatedly.

A podiatrist recommends that you dust the insides of your shoes with an antifungal powder or spray. There are several brands on the market, and they work just fine—and a lot faster than four weeks. Nevertheless, a homeopathic pharmacy suggests cotton dipped in raw honey and placed between the infected toes—but not in bed, please.

The fungus that causes athlete's foot dies in sunlight. So get those feet out under those rays for half an hour a day and, yes, while it may not be the easiest way, we back the old wives on this one: vinegar works.

GINGER ALE IS GOOD
FOR AN UPSET STOMACH

....

"A lot of indigestion is caused by people having to eat their own words." SCHOLAR ELYNN NICHOLSON

Can simple old ginger ale calm Mount Vesuvius while it's erupting in your stomach? We asked around.

Dr. Stephen Shaw told us that all ginger ale has some form of ginger root in it. Ginger is used in Chinese medicine as a strengthener for the stomach. It also has antibacterial effects that regulate the area around the solar plexus.

Ginger root ground up and brewed is more effective than ginger ale. Carbonation is not particularly friendly to the body. Although a carbonated beverage may provide some immediate relief by causing us to belch and release irritating gases, the carbonation also tends to bloat you. Its carbon dioxide permeates the membrane of the stomach, and goes into the bloodstream. The blood tries to get rid of the carbon dioxide through respiration or urination and this causes the body more trouble than its minimal relief to the stomach. Cold liquids also sedate the stomach and neutralize or dilute stomach acids, which then have to be rewarmed before they can be effective in digestion. Sucking on a ginger root or making chamomile tea has a much better effect on an upset stomach than ginger ale.

So, yes, ginger ale can be good for an upset stomach, but to get to the root of the problem, it's best to take your ginger straight up.

LETTING CHILDREN SUCK THEIR THUMBS WILL CAUSE BUCKTEETH

....

"I sucked my thumb until I was eleven." ROSANNA ARQUETTE

Is your child reminiscent of Linus in *Peanuts*, roaming around with a tattered blanket and his thumb stuck in his mouth? Do you have visions of him growing up to look like Bugs Bunny? Those fears may be justified. Orthodontists tell us that children who suck their thumbs or fingers usually stop by the age of three and a half to four. Before then there is no need to concern yourself, but from five to six years onward (when "adult" teeth start to come in) overbites and other dental problems can occur.

To stop thumb-sucking, there are various old-wife-approved methods. One is to apply various foul-smelling or foul-tasting concoctions to his child's finger. Another is wearing gloves. Keeping the thumbs busy at another task (piano lessons, etc.) is also very effective. As with many child-raising techniques, there is controversy. Some pediatricians think that thumb-sucking should just be ignored in older children, as long as it's only done while falling asleep or in the wake of emotion.

Yet most experts agree that from the age of four through the early teenage years, when the teeth, gums, and jaw structure are progressing through their most dramatic growth phases, parents should actively discourage their children from the habit.

But if your child does suck his thumb, that hardly makes him a freak. Research has shown that 61 to 87 percent of all infants and young children between birth and five suck either pacifiers, thumbs, or fingers at least for several months. Thumb-suckers are probably born, not made, as documented by numerous photos of fetuses in the womb already assuming the Linus position, although thumb-sucking may also start well after birth.

There is an ongoing debate and various opinions on *why* kids continue to suck their thumbs after five. Some experts say it's simply a learned behavior, others that it may indicate psychological problems. Many believe it signifies delayed emotional growth.

To the psychologists we say "chill out." We know lots of people whose emotional growth continues to be delayed, some who avoid it altogether. To our knowledge, none of these people have buckteeth, although a few still have their "Brady Bunch" lunch boxes.

SPINACH MAKES YOU STRONGER

"I yam what I yam." POPEYE

Raw spinach has become the nineties' "designer vegetable," and for good reason. It's loaded with potassium, iron, and other minerals essential for overall body conditioning. It has B vitamins too, which don't exactly make us strong, but are good for anxiety and the nervous system in general. So spinach may not "pump you up," but actually help to calm you down.

Spinach is relatively new as vegetables go. Its origins are in Persia and it traveled to Europe during the Moorish invasion of Spain. (The English then called spinach "that Spanish vegetable." Today kids call it "that yucky stuff.") There are two varieties: *smooth leaf* (used mostly in food processing) and *crumpled leaf* which we buy fresh at the market. Commercially grown spinach is mostly large and crinkled Bloomsdale, dark green and American.

Raw spinach is definitely rich in nutrients, but some authorities of a holistic bent advise that when we cook it the minerals oxidize and end up in a form the body can't absorb. They argue that boiling spinach seriously diminishes its value because the high temperature (110 degrees) kills all its natural enzymes. This forces our bodies to put up their own enzymes to digest the stuff, thus robbing us either way. They also feel that the type of iron found in spinach is especially difficult for the body to assimilate.

Everyone agrees that spinach is considerably more healthy than, say a pastrami sandwich or a half pint of Ben and Jerry's. A half cup of spinach provides about twice the vitamin A, and half the vitamin C that an adult requires daily. In addition, spinach ranks right up with that health-food veteran, brewer's yeast, as a source of folic acid.

So, no, spinach doesn't make you stronger, but it does have a beneficial effect on overall health. With all due respect to Popeye, though, try it raw.

CATS PURR WHEN THEY ARE HAPPY

"Cats are intended to teach us that not everything in nature has a purpose." GARRISON KEILLOR

One thing is for sure—cats *do* purr when they're contented. We humans call this happiness. But cats also purr when they're frightened or if they've been badly hurt. Purring is a spontaneous occurrence that may not have a clear emotional attachment.

Actually, it appears to be like a homing device. Within days, newborn cats hear the purr of their mothers and soon repeat it. This then becomes the mother cat's "radar" to home in on her baby. In fact, kittens learn how to purr before they can even see, hear, or smell. Conversely, as the mother cat purrs the vibration calls the kittens to nurse. Kittens can *feel* their way home to Mom.

Just *how* a cat purrs is up for debate. There are differing theories, one of which centers around a pair of "false vocal cords," a group of membranes that lie above the real vocal cords and seem to have no other function. Others believe that the motor sound of the purr originates in the thyroid apparatus, a series of small bones connecting the skull and the larynx that normally serves to support the tongue. The reason for this confusion is that cats rarely purr with a researcher's investigating spatula down their throat.

So purring originates as a signal from the mother cat, rather like ringing the triangle on the ranch, that it's time for the little'uns to head home. Later, purring occurs when cats feel they are just where they should be. It's not really whether they are happy or not that is the issue, although that's close. More specifically, purring is the cat's way of announcing that whether they are hungry or satisfied, healthy or in pain, at least they feel protected and at home.

YOU CAN CONTRACT AIDS FROM KISSING

"Life is a sexually transmitted disease." GUY BELLAMY

It wasn't that long ago that this *new* old wives' tale was widely believed. We now know more about how AIDS is transmitted and clearly it's not from casual hugging and kissing. Still, we are cautioned to be more discriminating, to stay aware and protect ourselves and others in every way we can, which includes getting tested for AIDS, requiring our partners to do the same, and practicing "safe sex."

It's hard on romance. But how does well-founded caution somehow turn into blind fear and paranoia, until finally everything seems dangerous? As comic Dennis Miller says, "I hear you can contract AIDS from hoping you don't get it."

But doesn't saliva count as one of those "bodily fluids" we hear so much about?

Here's what medicine tells us: with AIDS, some bodily fluids are a lot more dangerous than others. In fact, studies indicate that while the commingling of saliva that occurs during a deep kiss might in theory, be a risk, far less of the virus is contained in saliva than in blood, semen, or vaginal fluid. So although *it may be theoretically barely possible* to contract the disease orally, the mouth is not the most likely or hospitable place in the body for the AIDS virus. The immune-system cells of the anus and vagina are far more easily infected with HIV.

If the HIV virus were easily transmitted through saliva, a great many more of us would already be infected. And if all bodily fluids were equally dangerous, being on a crowded bus during cold season would rate as a high-risk activity. (Actually, it *is* a high-risk activity, but not because of AIDS.) The big fact is *there is not one case documented of anyone contracting the disease from kissing* or otherwise "swapping spit." So no need to run out for those new mouth-condoms.

As Harold Jaffee of the Centers for Disease Control in Atlanta so succinctly puts it: "If you get infected blood in your mouth, I'd be pretty worried. If you get semen in your mouth, there's some risk. If you get saliva in your mouth, it's got to be a very low risk."
Excerpt from *Newsweek* cover story, August 3, 1992.

Some additional information on AIDS:

TELLING CHILDREN ABOUT AIDS

AIDS is a scary topic for parents and children. But silence can be deadly. Straightforward talk is the best apporach. Here are some basic facts to keep in mind:

AIDS is hard to catch: There are only three major means of transmission: unprotected intercourse, the transfer of blood and passage from an infected mother to a baby during pregnancy or birth. Transfusions are not considered risky; since 1985, the blood supply has been screened for the AIDS virus:

There have been no known cases of infection from sneezing, toilet seats, dishes, drinking fountains, telephones or any other ordinary contact with someone who has AIDS.

The virus that causes AIDS can hide in the body for many years without developing into full-blown AIDS. Most carriers do not appear ill, and may not even know that they are infected. They can unknowingly pass on the virus.

AIDS is fatal. There is no cure for AIDS at the present time, although drugs help infected people live longer.

The only really safe sex is no sex. But sex is less risky if the man wears a latex condom and the couple uses spermicide containing nonoxynol-9, which provides additional protection. Check the condom to make sure there are no holes and look for the expiration date on the spermicide.

The skin is a barrier against germs, including the AIDS virus. However, it's possible—though unlikely—to be infected if the blood of an HIV-positive person gets into the body through cuts in the skin. Use latex gloves or other protection when touching other people's blood.

Traces of the AIDS virus have been detected in saliva, but experts say there is generally not enough HIV in saliva to spread the virus through kissing. A closed-mouth kiss is safe. French kissing with an infected person could be risky if there are cuts on the lips or gums. Oral sex is not safe; use a latex condom or dental dam (a rubber square available at medical-supply stores and family-planning clinics).

EYE COLOR IS FIXED AT BIRTH

"The eyes have it."

"Oh look!"
    When an infant is born everyone is eager to see who it resembles and what color eyes it has. But infant eye color can change.
    At birth the iris is blue or gray, indicating a scarcity of pigment on its surface. As the amount of pigment increases, the iris tends to become darker. By about six months eye color is true.
    Each child possesses two genes for eye color, one inherited from the mother, and one from the father. For a child to have blue eyes, for instance, a blue (recessive) gene must be inherited from one parent. Thus two brown-eyed parents can have a blue-eyed offspring if one of the two genes for eye color that each parent passes on is a recessive blue gene. Complicated, isn't it?
    So the answer is yes, the hue of your child's eyes is genetically determined at birth, but you'll have to wait a few months to find out what that color is. Until then you might as well enjoy the guessing game.

IF YOU SHAVE YOUR EYEBROWS OFF THEY WON'T GROW BACK

....

"My acting range? Left eyebrow raised, right eyebrow raised." ROGER MOORE

It's not that they won't grow back. It's just that they grow back v-e-r-y s-l-o-w-l-y.

Eyebrow hair will return just as surely as scalp hair—although maybe more erratically. All human hair goes through regular growing phases, but the duration of these phases depends upon where the hair is located. For example, a strand of hair on your scalp will go through a growing phase for several years, then enter a three-month rest period and fall out. At any given time, 10 to 20 percent of your scalp hairs are in the resting and falling-out stages. (As if bald men didn't have *enough* bad news!)

Eyebrow hairs grow for thirty to sixty days and then pass into the resting phase, which usually lasts for more than a hundred days. So at any given time, most of your eyebrow hairs are not growing. (This should be a relief to Andy Rooney). If you shave your eyebrows during this period of time, it may take *months* for them to replace themselves because only a select minority of the hairs will start growing back right away.

Eyebrow hairs also grow at a slower rate than other body hair. Scalp hair grows 0.014 inches per day but eyebrows grow only 0.005 inches per day. (Who stands there with the tape measure?) Therefore, under normal circumstances—and what's normal about shaving your eyebrows in the first place?—it could take six to eight months for your eyebrows to return to their normal appearance (which you were trying to change in the *first* place).

So if your eyebrows fall out (through treatment) or you are a teenager whose mother is "like totally freaked, man" because you gave in to an overpowering need to shave them off, rest assured that they will grow back—although you may look like something from "Star Trek" for a while. Live long and prosper.

PUTTING ASPIRIN OR SUGAR IN WATER WITH CUT FLOWERS EXTENDS THEIR LIFE

"Flowers are the sweetest things God ever made and forgot to put a soul into."   HENRY WARD BEECHER

This doesn't mean that flowers get headaches and have a sweet tooth, does it?

One florist said, "Oh, yes, we recommend sugar and aspirin." Some customers even put 7UP in with the sugar. Others say only warm water with roses—it appears to bring them to full bloom quicker.

If you look through a microscope at a plant you can see small green dots call chloroplasts. These contain chlorophyll, which makes the plant green. The "veins" in the plant contain cells called xylem and phloem. The xylem carries water within the plant and the phloem carries sugar. The plant gets water through its roots and absorbs light and carbon dioxide from the air and sun. The plant then mixes the carbon dioxide and water, which makes the plant's food. The old wives say adding aspirin and sugar to this routine alters the process and causes flowers to last a day or so longer.

So the old wives got this one right. A spoonful of sugar and a dose of aspirin does cause flowers to last longer, and if, as Emerson says, "earth laughs in flowers," this gesture may cause them to keep laughing for a while.

EATING GELATIN WILL MAKE YOUR NAILS GROW

"Jell-O is the clown of desserts."   MERRIT MALLOY

Gelatin is made from the hooves of cattle. Since a hoof is more or less analogous to a fingernail, it follows that eating gelatin might help nails grow, right? Unfortunately no. Besides, who would want nails as thick as cows' hooves anyhow? Think of the manicure bills.

Most of us still believe that eating Jell-O will strengthen our nails. Yet the experts say the most important factor is an overall healthy diet. In fact, nails are so indicative of the body's condition as a whole that physicians in underdeveloped countries examine them as a way of diagnosing an inadequate diet.

You say you're in pretty good health, but your nails lack a certain "oomph?" Then heed the words of Leslie Kenton, health and beauty editor of *Harper's Bazaar* and *Queen*, who suggests a plethora of foods including liver, cod liver oil (yum!), or, more palatably, a daily dose of carrot juice. Egg yolks, cabbage, muscle meats, and onions all supply vital sulphur amino acids. Hangnails can be minimized by making sure you are consuming enough folic acid and vitamin C. Also B-complex nutrients are vital for the long, strong "Madame Butterfly" look. "Healthy nails should not only be strong but flexible, smooth and rich pink in color," says Ms. Kenton. "If yours are not, the first thing to do is to upgrade your eating habits. Nails, like hair, need protein, B-complex vitamins, minerals, trace elements (particularly zinc, calcium, iodine, sulphur, and iron), and vitamin A."

For you fingernail fanatics, other suggestions are a weekly manicure and a goodly number of raw vegetables and protein, brewer's yeast plus one teaspoon of blackstrap molasses a day. And finally, six to eight kelp tablets taken with each meal.

On the other hand, maybe we're being too dismissive of this whole Jell-O thing. How can anything served in every hospital in the nation be bad for your nails? Would Bill Cosby steer us wrong? Jell-O certainly can't hurt us, and it's more fun than some other desserts. So go ahead, make a big Jell-O mold for Aunt May's potluck dinner. However, the truly manicure-obsessed among you may want to throw in some carrots, egg yolk, blackstrap molasses, and a few kelp tablets. Your nails will never look better and you'll be certain to have plenty left to take home with you!

WOMEN HAVE ONE OR TWO MORE RIBS THAN MEN

"In passing, also, I would like to say that the first time Adam had a chance he laid the blame on women." LADY ASTOR

Since the beginning of time, people have been muttering about God dispensing an extra breastbone to females and we thought it finally deserved some investigation. It all started in the Bible— Eve was supposedly made from Adam's rib—but wait a minute.

Everyone has twelve ribs. Go ahead, count 'em.

The ancient Sumerians told a story about a consortium of gods who were busily turning the land of Dilmun into a paradise when one of their number, Enki the water god, committed a breach of etiquette by nibbling on a newly created plant. Ninhursag, the earth goddess, put a curse on Enki, and he fell ill as eight of his vital organs failed. Ninhursag was eventually persuaded to relent, but to cure Enki she had to create eight different new deities to cure each one of Enki's ailing organs. The story bears some resemblance to the Hebrew myth: the creation, the eating of the forbidden fruit, etc. But what is interesting is that the Hebrew name "Eve" means "she who makes live." In Sumerian, the word for "make live" is also their word for rib. Thus the name of the goddess created to cure Enki's aching rib, "Nin-Ti," becomes a Sumerian pun, meaning both "the lady of the rib" and "the lady who makes live."

So maybe the old wives who passed this one on came from Sumeria. In any case, this tale is false—they were ribbing us.

JEWISH MEN MAKE GOOD HUSBANDS

"Anybody who thinks marriage is a fifty-fifty proposition doesn't understand women or fractions." ANONYMOUS

A little boy comes home from synagogue and announces to his mother that he has just gotten a part in the school play—as a Jewish husband. "Now you march right back there," his mother demands, "and tell them you want a *speaking* part."

Old jokes and older stereotypes aside, the belief that Jewish men make better mates is widespread—and not only in the Jewish community. Women of all creeds and colors seem to believe that sons of David are more responsible, less likely to abuse alcohol, and more likely to treat women with their due respect. (Presumably the result of having received a thorough breaking-in at the hands of their Jewish mothers.)

We need only look at the media to see how these stereotypes are propagated. Ironically, the current image of the Jewish male is exemplified by Woody Allen. (And, as we all now know, whatever may be true of Mr. Allen's off-screen life, the words "ideal mate" no longer spring easily to mind.)

Regardless, the general image is of a sensitive, intelligent, and nonthreatening, if neurotic, man who is likely to treat the women in his life with a combination of awe and befuddlement, which is a lot better than being in a relationship with, say, Al Bundy or Joey Buttafuoco.

Well, what we've found are many opinions, some of them expert, but not a great wealth of hard data. For example, we were able to pin down a couple of psychologists from local universities (who preferred to remain nameless for fear of actually being held to their opinions) who told us that they felt that, in general, Jewish men are more affectionate and respectful of women. Similarly, ethnicity expert Dr. Andrei Simic of the University of Southern California subscribes to the same general picture of Jewish men, but also notes that some consider Jewish men to be "overbearing and dictatorial." He explains that Jews are not a single ethnic group, but actually a collection of several different ethnic and cultural groups under the umbrella of a single religion, and that Jewish "national character" might well vary between European, Syrian, or Sephardic Jews.

We've all heard how Jewish men drink less than others, and a number of small studies have been conducted over the last forty years which seem to support this view. For example, a survey of arrests for "Drunkenness" and "Under the Influence" by the New Haven, Connecticut police in 1951 showed Jews with by far the lowest rate in actual numbers of arrests relative to their population. Theories abound as to why Jews may be less prone to alcoholism, mostly relating to the use of wine in religious rituals and it's integration into normal family life and long-held beliefs encouraging moderation.

Similarly, Jewish law has historically strongly condemned the abuse of women. "One deserves greater punishment for striking his wife than for striking another person, for he is enjoined to respect her. Far be it from a Jew to do such a thing," wrote nineteenth-century jurist Rabbi Meir of Rothenberg. However, A 1983 study by Betsy Giller and Ellen Goldsmith of Hebrew Union College examined family violence among members of Los Angeles area synagogues. They found that the problem is significantly greater than is generally believed. Giller and Goldsmith theorize that because physical abuse is so strongly condemned as well as being thought of as an "unjewish" problem, the level of denial and fear of public exposure may be greater for troubled Jewish families than for others.

So, the facts remain intriguing, but hard to pin down. But we do know that the Talmud instructs "A man must love his wife as himself and honor her more than himself." *Any* man, Jew or not, who followed that advice would make a better-than-average mate.

APRICOT PITS CONTAIN CYANIDE

"I got food poisoning today. I don't know when I'm going to use it." STEPHEN WRIGHT

Yes, this is true.

Actually all fruits of the rose family—cherries, apples, plums, almonds (bitter), peaches, apricots, and crab apples—contain small amounts of cyanogenetic glycosides, which release hydrogen cyanide gas through an enzymatic reaction when eaten. Apricot pits are more lethal, having caused several cases of fatal poisoning.

A good guideline is simply to avoid apricot pits. Fortunately, suble-thal doses of cyanide gas are detoxified and passed out of the body rapidly, so it's impossible to slowly poison yourself over a period of time. Symptoms of cyanide poisoning are excitement, convulsions, respiratory distress, and spasms. Roasting kills the enzymes that pro-duce the lethal reaction without changing the mineral content of the food, but we won't be eating any apricot pits, cooked or otherwise!

Laetrile, a substance derived from apricot pits, was very popular a few years back as a supposed cure for cancer. Clinics (outside the United States, where it's illegal to administer) were touting this treat-ment along with an assortment of other "alternative" cures. But lae-trile not only doesn't stop cancer deaths, it may even hasten death in large doses because of the awesome toxicity of the cyanide.

So heed the old wives.

URINATING AFTER SEX PREVENTS BLADDER INFECTIONS

"Always make water when you can." DUKE OF WELLINGTON

Romantic, huh?

It's a rather indelicate subject, but there is evidence to show it is a good idea for women to run to the powder room after a particularly aggressive bout in bed . . . or even a brief interlude. The reasons are painfully real.

A third of all women between the ages of twenty and forty suffer from recurring urinary tract infections (UTI), the worst being cystitis. Women are more vulnerable because of their design. The female urethra—the tube that vents urine from the bladder—is much shorter than the male's. That means bacteria need only make a quick stroll from a woman's bladder to her kidneys! The pushing motion of sexual intercourse sometimes forces the bacteria upward, account-ing for outbreaks of "honeymoon cystitis." Cystitis is also likely dur-ing the later months of pregnancy. (That would be "posthoneymoon cystitis.")

The watchword here is frequency. In one test, women who repressed the "urge" to go for a significant duration were found to be more susceptible to infections. Especially significant is that women who did develop infection also refrained from relieving the bladder after sex. When these same women altered this one habit, most of them did not suffer any further infection.

So women are well advised to urinate just after sex. We know it's neither convenient nor very romantic, but a bladder infection is even less so. Also avoid chemical irritants such as perfumed sprays, bubble baths, and scented powders. To prevent infection altogether, drink lots of good old H_2O (six to eight glasses a day).

You know, we hate to say this, but sometimes matters of hygiene and health are not romantic. *At least not yet.* We suspect that during the next decade the two will (finally) coincide.

A CHANGE IN WEATHER AFFECTS PEOPLE WITH ARTHRITIS

· ·

"I've reached that age where a good day is one when you get up and nothing hurts." MERRIT MOLLOY'S GRANDMOTHER

Thirty-seven million Americans suffer from arthritis. Would they really be better off in warm, dry climates?

The Arthritis Foundation reminds us to make a clear distinction between weather and climate. "Weather" is the condition of the atmosphere at a given time (including temperature, humidity, and barometric pressure). "Climate" refers to the typical weather in a certain area over a long and definite period of time.

People can generally be classed into weather-sensitive and weather-insensitive groups based on the ease with which it affects their condition. So some, but not all, will be sensitive to weather and experience an increase of aches and pains during atmospheric changes. That's worth emphasizing: it's the change in conditions rather than the highness of humidity or lowness of barometric pressure per se that is responsible for the worsening symptoms. Unfortunately, right now nobody seems to know why this happens; they only know that it does.

As regards climate, that too seems to impact aches and pains. Just as the old wives suspected, some patients felt a benefit when in a controlled environment (a constant 90 degrees Fahrenheit with a 35 percent relative humidity). Moreover, it is true that physicians don't report many patients with crippling cases of arthritis in the Southwest. Patients in the dry desert climates of Arizona, New Mexico, and southern California do report feeling better than when they lived in the (far moister) middle and eastern regions of the United States.

So, yes, it looks like perhaps climate *and* weather can wreak their own havoc with arthritis. The old wives (and the old *ex*-wives) got it right this time.

A KISS UNDER THE MISTLETOE IS LUCKY

....

"I don't know how to kiss, or I would kiss you. Where do the noses go?" INGRID BERGMAN(TO GARY COOPER) IN *FOR WHOM THE BELL TOLLS*

Hanging mistletoe is one of our friendliest customs. It encourages us to be just a little sweeter to each other. So where did the custom come from?

According to Norse mythology, the goddess Frigg was so happy when her son Balder came back to life that her tears turned into pearls on the mistletoe. Because of this miracle, the mistletoe was placed under her protection, thereby preventing it from ever being used for evil purposes. Since Frigg is the goddess of love and marriage, kissing under her mistletoe involves protection for that love.

The mistletoe plant itself is a parasite of sorts that springs from seeds deposited by birds on the bark of trees. The woody "sinkers" insert into the host plant, from which it derives sustenance. It's said that the most magical of all mistletoe grows on oak trees. According to legend, the plant is to be cut with a gold knife or sickle. Don't let mistletoe touch the ground, or it will lose its magical powers.

The custom of kissing under the mistletoe came from the folklore of fertility practices. A woman kissed under the mistletoe was assured of fertility. Mistletoe is still customarily used as a protection against evil.

The branches of mistletoe used to be attached to the doors of newlyweds to bring them happiness. We are warned never to take all the boughs off a mistletoe plant or it will bring bad luck. Legend also has it that if one hangs mistletoe in a tree with a swallow's wing, all the cuckoos in the area will assemble there.

Today we still believe that any unmarried girl who stands under a mistletoe and does not get kissed will not be married that year. And if she *refuses* to be kissed, she will die an old maid, thus robbing us of one more old wife to tell these tales.

NEVER SQUEEZE A BOIL

"Things forbidden have a secret charm." TACITUS

To squeeze or not to squeeze.

Many believe that a boil is an external manifestation of an internal problem, but these are the facts: Boils (as distinguished from pimples, which have a variety of causes and are *much* less painful) are created by staphylococcus bacteria invading through a break in the skin and infecting a blocked oil gland or hair follicle. The body's immune system sends in white blood cells to kill the invaders and the battle creates a red inflammation and debris which is the pus. A pus-filled abscess begins to grow beneath the skin surface, rising up red and painful. Sometimes the body reabsorbs the boil; other times the boil swells to an eruption, drains, and subsides.

Boils *can* be dangerous. If the bacteria from a boil gets into the bloodstream, it can cause blood poisoning. So don't squeeze it since you may end up breaking it inward into your bloodstream, rather than outward as would occur naturally. It is said to be dangerous to squeeze a boil around your lips or nose because of proximity to the brain. In fact, it may be marginally more dangerous because the surrounding skin is weaker and so blood poisoning may occur more easily. It is certainly more painful. Doctors advise getting help if there are red lines radiating from the boil or if you have fever or chills or swelling of lymph nodes.

The traditional treatment for boils is heat. A warm compress should be held over the boil for twenty to thirty minutes three to four times a day. This brings healing in five to seven days.

91

A poultice of milk, salt, and flour heated together is a well-known natural remedy; the skin of a hard-boiled egg draws pus out and relieves the inflammation of a boil; also, slices of pumpkin can be applied directly to bring the boil to a head. Other old wives' remedies include poultices made from minced or raw chopped garlic, heated lemons, or roasted figs, raw onion, the outer leaves of cabbage, a bag of black tea, and a variety of herbs.

In any case, if there is no sign of spreading infection after the boil has come to a natural head, medics recommend taking a sterilized needle and making a small nick in the head. Sometimes nature needs a helping hand.

GINSENG MAKES YOU MORE VIRILE

"One night I made love for an hour and five minutes. It was the day they pushed the clock ahead." GARRY SHANDLING

Mankind has always searched for an actual aphrodisiac. Does ginseng do the trick?

Japanese and Korean hospitals use ginseng extract to treat impotence. In the lab, ginseng was found to contain sex hormone substances. The Japanese found that testicular RNA and DNA levels did increase after several doses of ginseng. Yet injections of such hormones into healthy males does not seem to really improve sex drive. So we think the scientific evidence that ginseng is effective is very weak. On the other hand, hope springs eternal (and sometimes with it other things).

There are four different kinds of ginseng: American, Siberian, Chinese, and Korean. American ginseng has a "cool" property, is not thermal, and therefore is thought only to have a somewhat heating effect on the sex organs. It is used for lung and stomach problems. Chinese ginseng is "warmer" than the American variety. It is used as an antioxidant in the bloodstream and the product Gensana is made from it. It is supposed to help with virility as well as promoting healthy lungs. Siberian ginseng is used for tinctures as an antioxidant and for digestion. It is regarded as having some effect on virility as well. Korean ginseng, or *red* ginseng, tends to be very "hot" and stimulating. Practitioners say it induces sweating and heavy stimulation of the sexual organs, promoting erection and staying power to prolong the sex act.

Ginseng is a root called Radix Panax. You can grind it into a powder and brew it into tea, or you can make an extract of it using alcohol and/or water. Taken regularly, its advocates say you should notice increased virility in approximately one to two weeks. Many of them feel very confident of this. But, they warn, watch out for side effects— restlessness, night sweats, emotional irritation. Also erections during business hours can be a problem. (Isn't that sort of what you were hoping for?) Please note that those suffering from high blood pressure should beware.

So ginseng may be somewhat effective as an aphrodisiac drug. It sometimes works wonders on the mind.

BINDING FEET KEEPS THEM SMALL

"The custom and fashion of today will be the awkwardness and outrage of tomorrow—so arbitrary are these transient laws." ALEXANDER DUMAS

The answer is a sad and painful yes. Imagine the Jolly Green Giant trying to fit into Minnie Mouse's shoes. OUCH!

This grotesque practice began in China in the tenth century, just before the Sung Dynasty, as a fashion among the palace dancers. It consists of wrapping young girls feet with bandages so that their feet cannot grow. As the foot tries to grow, but is held in place by the bandages, it becomes gnarled—and very painful both for the girl as she grows, and for the grown woman if she tries to walk. The irony is that crippled women cannot dance, so imperial China lost its rich tradition of classical dance.

Later the binding became tighter, and the bound foot came to be known as a status symbol, indicating that a woman was able to go through life doing little but hobbling, and in turn needed to be carried over any but the shortest distances. This proved she was clearly not of the laboring classes, nor was she likely to stray far from her proper place as an ornament of her husband's house. The custom then spread to the poorer sections of the Chinese culture as well.

Over the centuries these strange, distorted limbs became a national fetish. By virtue of its very secrecy, swathed from sight in the bandages that compressed it, the foot became a symbol of all that was most intimate. Erotic prints from the Sung and Ming periods show women naked in every respect except their feet. In fact, in grown women, bound feet cannot be unwrapped without considerable risk and enormous pain caused by blood rushing into constricted blood vessels which are not strong enough in this area to withstand sudden pressure and are therefore very likely to burst.

For centuries there were campaigns against this disabling custom. From the start of the Ch'ing dynasty the Manchus tried to abolish it, and they prohibited it within Manchu families. Yet even imperial edicts failed to have any effect on the now deeply ingrained habit. Only in the late nineteenth century, when activists rose up and formed natural-foot societies, was any progress made. It was one of those causes to which European and American ladies eagerly devoted their energies, and it became part of a wider crusade for the general emancipation of women, and indeed for the modernization of China.

Suddenly, in the opening years of the twentieth century, the age-old custom began to disappear at quite a remarkable speed, swept away by progress and enlightenment and the same forces that would bring to an end the Ch'ing dynasty and more than two thousand years of imperial history.

The old wives were always rightly opposed to foot-binding. It had the tragic effect of tricking an entire culture of women into diminishing themselves.

TAKE THAT MAKEUP OFF BEFORE YOU GO TO SLEEP OR YOU WILL RUIN YOUR SKIN

"It is a folly to expect people to do all that they may reasonably be expected to do." ARCHBISHOP WHATELY

It's late. You're tired. You look in your bathroom mirror, thrust a toothbrush into your mouth, and sigh. You're just too exhausted to go through the whole ritual of removing your makeup. You say to yourself, "One night won't make a difference," and flop into bed. Have you just betrayed your skin?

Makeup is a great barrier during the day, protecting us from the elements, dirt, and dehydrating winds. But if not totally removed at night it can clog pores, initiating all kinds of problems.

Under your skin are tiny organs called the sebaceous glands that secrete oil to maintain lubrication of the surface above and seal in moisture. Dry climates, the environment, and aging can exacerbate skin dryness, as can long, hot baths.

Cleansing the skin serves two purposes—getting rid of excess oils and washing away dead, dry cells (exfoliation) that need to be removed consistently so the skin continues to look youthful. For women over thirty-five, for whom cell production and the rate of exfoliation have slowed, proper cleaning can make all the difference. Some skin experts recommend cleansing twice a day, morning and night. Sweat, oils, and toxins quickly build. If you are rushed, splash your face with warm water to rehydrate.

The skin is assaulted daily in many ways—with sun, blemishes, and environmental factors we don't control. Taking makeup off at night really makes sense.

CHARCOAL HELPS FLATULENCE

"Indigestion is charged by God with enforcing morality on the stomach." VICTOR HUGO

A ll right, you know about beans. But there is a whole list of other foods that can induce flatulence. The list varies from person to person. The symptoms usually appear within one to four hours after eating particular foods. The foods which are particularly suspect are apples, brussels sprouts, broccoli, cabbage, carbonated beverages, cauliflower, dairy products, diet foods with sorbitol, onions, radishes, and, of course, beans.

The bean has sugars that can't be broken down by the digestive system. Mixed with microbes in the colon, the result is, well, uncomfortable and often embarrassing. Yet there is great news about beans. Evidence has shown that if you soak beans overnight and boil them in fresh water with an onion, you reduce "the problem."

History tells us that a Frenchman, Joseph Pujol (a.k.a. Le Petomane), earned twenty thousand francs a week in vaudeville from 1887 to 1914 by performing world-class flatulence sounds, including impressions, and actually flatulating popular tunes of the day. Where did he get all this gas?

You can get gas from air that you swallow. As you eat and drink you actually swallow air with your food. Some of us gulp our food down like an express train and a few hours later regret it. Try using a straw for your (noncarbonated) drink and eating more slowly. A strong cup of peppermint tea can give you relief very quickly, and a "hot water compress" placed directly on the stomach can also relieve gas pains. The old home remedy of eating a raw onion sandwich is the quintessential "bite of the dog that bit you" remedy.

The good news is, yes, activated charcoal *is* effective at absorbing gas. It can be obtained in pill form. But beware—it should be taken only occasionally, not daily, as it may absorb more than gas (i.e. vitamins, minerals, etc.).

WASH YOUR HAIR EVERY DAY AND YOU'LL NEVER GET DANDRUFF!

Frequent washing is no cure but it does make the dandruff a little easier to control. A mild shampoo is enough. But what causes dandruff?

It's mostly due to an overly oily scalp. Shampooing regularly with a mild shampoo diluted with an equal amount of distilled water can control the oil without aggravating your scalp. You may need a medicated shampoo with "active ingredients." These products contain selenium sulfide or zinc pyrithione, which are pretty effective. They slow the rabbitlike rate at which the scalp cells multiply. Other ingredients like salicylic acid and sulfur loosen flakes so they can be washed away easily. The products with antibacterial agents can reduce further the already very small chance of infection on the scalp. Some hair aficionados recommend tar-based shampoos. They also retard cell growth (although you must leave them on for five to ten minutes). Some of the newer brands have more pleasant aromas; you may want to alternate them with your regular shampoo if you find them too harsh.

Even though excess oil causes dandruff, your hair may benefit from a hot oil treatment, which loosens and softens dandruff scales. Olive oil is good, too. Sunlight in moderation (only thirty minutes or so) also may help. Direct ultraviolet light has an anti-inflammatory effect on scaly skin conditions.

A natural remedy is thyme. It is purported to have antiseptic properties that can help alleviate dandruff.

An Arabian remedy is to wash your hair in a combination of one cup of beet juice and two cups of water plus one teaspoon of salt. (Do not try this if you have light-colored hair.) Also, don't forget the trusty juice of lemons. Apply half to your hair. Mix the other half with two cups of water. Wash your hair with mild shampoo, then rinse again with lemon and water mixture. Continue every other day until dandruff is gone.

So washing your hair may help rid you of annoying dandruff. It will do so more effectively and faster if you use an anti-dandruff shampoo. Don't dismay. Dandruff is controllable. Losing your hair is not.

IF YOU GRIND YOUR TEETH AT NIGHT YOUR TEETH WILL WEAR DOWN

"Some tortures are physical and some are mental, but the one that is both is dental." OGDEN NASH

Nocturnal noshers who grind their teeth while sleeping (a condition commonly called bruxism) can expect headaches, sore necks, and bad backs as well as a host of conditions known as temporomandibular joint syndrome (TMJ). Yes, they are also likely to suffer worn-down teeth (and spouses).

Of course the main culprit is stress. Anxious grinding and angered clenching are primal instincts. Whatever the root cause, the sufferers are unaware that they're doing it. They are sleeping peacefully— except for the constant munching, which grinds their tooth enamel like cornmeal.

But wait, there's help. First of all keep your teeth apart when you're awake. Your teeth should touch only when you are chewing or swallowing. If you practice keeping your teeth apart then it will reduce the urge to grind them together later. Unfortunately, this is akin to "trying not to think of a monkey"—difficult.

Another thing you can do is give your jaws a workout during the day by crunching some carrots, celery, or an apple. Or try a mouth guard, like boxers wear; this can reduce nighttime chomping. You can find them at sports stores or have your doctor custom-make one for you.

To alleviate discomfort, heat can be applied to your jaw. Hot washcloths or a heating pad on low are recommended. Some noted natural cures are chewable calcium supplements, bone meal tablets, and wheat germ.

To counteract stress, give up caffeine in all its various forms. Take a warm bath with relaxing oils before going to sleep. Relaxation exercises, yoga, and tai chi are also wise practices.

If your life has really become a daily (or nightly) grind, we strongly suggest that you consult with your doctor. As Snoopy would contend, when your bite is off, so is your bark.

BUTTER HEALS A BURN

This time the old wives are dead wrong.

Other old-time folk remedies include vinegar, potato scrapings, and honey. If you put all these supposed salves together you might have a really weird dessert, but they won't do a burn any good. In fact oily matter, by holding heat closer to the skin, might worsen the injury at least to some very slight degree.

Instead, *cold water* seems to be the best immediate response. "The first and most important thing is to stop the burning process," says emergency medicine specialist Dr. William P. Burdick. "Flush the burns with lots of cold water—fifteen to thirty minutes' worth or until the burning stops. But don't use ice or ice water—they can make the burn worse. Once you've put the fire out, you're halfway to healing. The coolness stops the burning from spreading through your tissue and works as a temporary painkiller." Then there are several anti-burn salves on the market which manufacturers claim do good things, and we have no reason to disagree.

Of course, some burns are too severe for self-treatment. The rule of thumb is to consult a doctor if a first- or second-degree burn is larger than a silver dollar or if the burned person is over sixty or under a year old.

You should loosely wrap the burn in a clean, dry cloth such as a thick gauze pad and then leave it alone for about a day; the healing process should be allowed to begin on its own. Once twenty-four hours have passed you should wash your injury once a day gently with soap and water or a mild Betadine solution and be sure to keep it covered, dry, and clean between cleansings.

One ancient homeopathic remedy that actually works is aloe vera. Two or three days after your burn, break open a fresh piece of aloe and spread the plant's natural moisture on the affected area, or squeeze on an over-the-counter 100 percent aloe cream. Both have a soothing effect on the burn. (Don't use aloe if you are using blood thinners or have a medical history of heart problems.) Remember, any blisters that form should be left intact. "Those bubbles of skin are nature's own best bandage," says a burn specialist. If a blister pops, you should wash it with soap and water, followed by an antibiotic ointment and a bandage. As the burn starts to heal, you can break open a capsule of vitamin E and rub the liquid onto your irritated skin. It will feel good and may prevent scarring.

Of course, you can go the traditional route with the old wives and try plastering potato scrapings and scads of butter and vinegar on your burns. While you're at it, throw on some chives.

COLD WEATHER, CHILLS, AND WET FEET CAUSE COLDS

....

"The only thing harder to get rid of than a winter cold is a 1973 Ford Pinto." AILEEN FOSTER

How many times have you seen characters on television with their feet in hot water and a towel over their heads, sniffling up a storm? Immediately you know they have a cold. But have you ever tried this yourself? (Personally, we've never seen anybody do this, but then, we've never seen a drunk at a party with a lampshade on his head either.) So what causes the dreaded common cold? Down through the ages, the old wives blamed it on cold weather, "catching a chill," and wet feet.

Three decades of research have done a pretty good job of undermining the old wives on the matter. Colds are viruses and are therefore caused by contact with people who have them—not by drafts, chills, wet weather, or any other environmental factor. In fact, cold viruses are more likely to be killed off in the cold.

Still, in one public opinion poll, 64 percent of those surveyed believed that colds were caused by cold weather. It's understandable. Colds certainly seem to propagate in chilly weather, but the correlation is far from direct. Colds tend to peak in frequency during the cool autumn months, decrease in the early days of winter, peak again after New Years' (probably due to holiday partying), and then decline once more. Such evidence would certainly seem to partially support the correlation between cold weather and cold viruses.

But, of course, it doesn't. The reason colds seem to increase in the winter is that we infect each other more because we all crowd together in warm but relatively unventilated rooms instead of fishing or playing golf in the great outdoors—or at least opening a window.

So don't worry. Getting wet or getting your feet cold won't give you a cold. Eskimos and Olympic swimmers don't get any more colds than do other folks.

THE NUMBER 13 IS UNLUCKY

"Some people are alarmed if the company are thirteen in number. The number is only to be dreaded when the dinner is provided but for twelve." LANCELOT STURGEON

Friday the 13th: Whether the movie or the day, it inspires fear and sometimes terror.

Very few hotels have a thirteenth floor, the number thirteen is rarely seen in any elevators, and you'll notice no thirteen in the addresses of shopping complexes. Airlines avoid the number thirteen for their flights and seat numbers.

This, like many other bizarre superstitions, came from an interpretation of the Bible. At the Last Supper, Christ sat down with his twelve apostles. Even today, when one has a party of thirteen people then, according to this tradition, it is held that one member of that group will die within the year. The first to arise from Christ's last table was Judas, the betrayer, and we know he wasn't getting up to wash his hands.

Thirteen is also the traditional number of a coven of witches, and thirteen covens form a larger group. (If you're a witch you're probably not bothered much about bad luck.)

Conversely, there's a lot of symbolism suggesting *good* luck for the number thirteen. On the back of the dollar bill, the Great Seal of the United States contains a pyramid of thirteen steps. However, considering what has happened to the value of a dollar, that may *prove* thirteen brings bad luck! There are thirteen leaves and berries on the olive branch. The eagle holds thirteen arrows to represent the original colonies. And if you're a Jewish boy or girl at thirteen you can count your fortune in pens at your bar or bat mitzvah.

Most people don't really believe this bunk around the number thirteen, yet we've noticed that neither do they take any undue risks if Friday happens to fall on the 13th.

VITAMIN SUPPLEMENTS WORK

"If I had known I was going to live this long, I'd have taken better care of myself." Eubie Blake

The controversy rages.

Some experts maintain that a balanced diet eliminates any need for vitamin supplements. Then there are those who stress that our food has been depleted of nutrients by chemicals and that vitamins are *essential* to fortifying our immune system against the onslaught of pollution and stress.

No one disagrees that vitamins are essential. The debate is in what amount. The government issues figures on minimum daily requirements and the medical community splits on the debate over more or less. Since most vitamins cannot be made by the body, we must supply them in the diet or with supplements. The vitamins— including A, the B complex, C, D, E, and K—are involved in the continual process of repair and maintenance of the body's tissues. Vitamin deficiencies have profound medical consequences. Such deficiency-caused diseases as scurvy or beriberi are rare in the West, but not in underdeveloped countries.

Most vitamins, especially D and A, can cause problems when taken in excessive amounts. A possible exception to this is vitamin C, and indeed some very respected scientists believe that large doses of C are beneficial in warding off infections.

According to *Prevention* magazine, additional vitamins can help or even cure a plethora of illnesses. Vitamin A is credited with helping arthritis, kidney stones, night vision, and warts. Vitamin B is thought to reduce depression, hangovers, shingles, wrinkles, asthma, and carpal tunnel syndrome, while vitamin C can help with bruises, canker sores, diabetes, emphysema, gingivitis, etc.

So there is evidence that extra vitamins may help us but, in overly high doses, harm us as well. Be sure to check with your doctor, pharmacist, or nutritionist to ensure the right dosages for you.

LOW READING LIGHT WILL MAKE YOU GO BLIND

"All my good reading, you might say, was done in the toilet .... There are passages of Ulysses *which can be read only in the toilet—if one wants to extract the full flavor of their content."* HENRY MILLER

"Don't read in the dark, you'll go blind," our parents all warned. And over 50 percent of the population wears glasses. Are we to assume they *all* defied their parents?

Yes—but that's not the cause of poor vision. Reading in low light is annoying and tiring, but it doesn't seriously damage our vision. On the other hand, poor *contrast* does lead to eyestrain. A soft, low-glare light that provides high contrast seems to be best for reducing eye fatigue. The trick here is *placement* of the light. The big mistake is to place the light *in front* of the reader, causing light to shine directly in the eyes. Placing the light source to the side is good, as is common overhead light.

So why do so many people have trouble with their vision? Only 2 or 3 percent of the population have eye problems at birth. We note authors Kavner and Dusky: "Man's eyes evolved to direct us as we walked through the forests and over mountains, trapping animals and planting grain. Eyes were made to look at sunsets and horizons. Today we barely give them a chance to do anything but concentrate on the details." They might have added that eyes were only meant to last thirty or forty years because by that time our legs would have given out and we would have been caught by some wandering dinosaur. No wonder, now that dinosaurs rarely bother us and some of us even live on until Willard Scott takes notice, that our eyes often give out along the way.

So what can we do about it? One suggestion is to interrupt your work at least every few hours. Go look at something else—the horizon, a human face—it matters only that you give your eyes a break. Just reducing the brightness of your computer monitor can lower the stress level on the eyes.

Author Meir Schneider credits yoga with restoring his nearly lost eyesight, which is now 20/60 and still improving. Another new-agey solution for eyestrain is soaking your eyes in towels (ten to fifteen minutes) saturated with something called eyebright tea—an herb concoction found in health food stores. The simplest way to relieve eyestrain is simply to rest your eyes. One doctor says, "When you're on the phone, if you don't need to read or write, just close your eyes while you're talking. Depending on how much time you spend on the phone each day, you may be able to rest your eyes for as much as an hour or two." Eye problems may be a result of low physical condition; a sedentary lifestyle can affect the eyes just as much as close work. So odd as it sounds, if you want to improve your eyes try taking a walk around the block. You may not only see better; you just might feel better, too.

IF YOU USE TAMPONS YOU CAN LOSE YOUR VIRGINITY

"I understand that the majority of the romantic poetry is odes to dead virgins. Now, that's the darnedest thing. What would anyone do with a dead virgin?" ANNE WILSON SCHAEF

The usual definition of a virgin is someone who hasn't had sex yet. Simple, really. And few of us would argue that using a tampon in any way constitutes sex. But issues of virginity are historically biased and confused.

Just be grateful you didn't get your period during the Stone Age, when women were sent to the "menstrual hut." Made from leaves and bark, this tiny room protected the tribe from the "evil" menstrual blood. Tribesmen thought that menstruating women could ruin food, crops, or water simply by their touch. To have contact with or even look at a menstruating woman was considered bad luck, even a crime. Then, just to add icing to the misogynist cake, women were punished if their periods lasted longer than four or five days. It seems their absence also harmed the crops! (No wonder they demanded the vote.) Even today, primitive tribes in Africa and Brazil isolate their women in a separate building during their periods.

The (supposedly) enlightened Greeks and Romans believed that women having their periods could turn wine sour, dry up gardens, rust bronze, or dull steel with just one touch of a hand. Perhaps this was an early description of PMS.

Yet there is (almost) as much misunderstanding today about menstruation as in ancient times. A lot of girls have been advised not to exercise during their period, though exercise improves blood circulation and relieves cramps. And, yes, some women still believe that a tampon can cause them to lose their virginity.

The confusion here centers around the hymen. (Some things never change.) For you uninitiated out there, the hymen is a weblike piece of skin that partially blocks the opening to the vagina—until *something* breaks it. Gynecologists tell us that a tampon inserted normally will not rupture the hymen.

In the past, when the double standard ruled, the unbroken hymen was used as a "proof" of virginity. But strenuous exercise, particularly horseback riding, has been known to tear the hymen, yet no sex is involved (unless you're a strict Freudian). Happily sheets are no longer inspected the morning after a wedding night (as was the practice during medieval times) to ensure that the bride had been previously untouched. If you were unlucky enough to be the new wife of Henry VIII and had a penchant for horseback riding (nonsidesaddle), it could have been off with your head! Or a few centuries earlier . . . back to the hut!

CATS CAN SUCK THE BREATH
OUT OF A NEWBORN

. . . .

"God bless this house but not the cat." IRISH PROVERB

Felines have always suffered from bad press—as witches' "familiars," or when black as harbingers of bad luck—so the idea of killer kitties fits right in. An old medical textbook claims that cats had been observed with their mouths open over infant corpses.

Today we more readily blame sudden infant death syndrome (SIDS), which is defined as the unexplained death of a baby under one year of age. In the United States, about eight thousand deaths per year, mostly of children under six months of age, are attributed to SIDS.

Although several theories have been put forward by pediatricians and pathologists, no one is certain of the syndrome's cause. Many researchers believe it has to do with the suppression of normal breathing in the central nervous system. Honey contaminated with botulism is thought to be one cause. (For that reason, honey is not recommended for babies under the age of one year.) Not quite as farfetched as the killer cats, but still erroneous, was the belief in the 1920s and '30s that sudden infant deaths were linked to an excessively large thymus. We now know that the thymus actually *shrinks* in size during times of stress or illness.

So both cats and thymuses are acquitted.

However, we are definitely not recommending that you throw your cat in the bassinet as a playmate for your newborn. Cats have a penchant for snuggling up close to people and, while improbable, it's not quite inconceivable that they could inadvertently smother an infant who is too young to push the cat away.

DRINKING ALCOHOL ON A PLANE FLIGHT AGGRAVATES JET LAG

"I don't mind hecklers, because I know how to ignore people—I was an airline stewardess." JO-ANN DEERING

P lanes are safer than cars, and it's a lot less dangerous to drink and fly than to drink and drive unless you're the pilot, of course. But this isn't meant in any way to encourage drinking on airline flights.

Airplane cabins are very dry and, although drinking helps combat dehydration, booze is not the liquid experts recommend. Alcohol's diuretic action dehydrates you. Juice, soda, or mineral water are clearly the best choices.

What about caffeine? It's also a diuretic, but caffeine can actually help counteract jet lag. Experiments show that caffeine can be used to reset our internal body clocks. One plan that frequent travelers suggest is to cut out caffeine a day or two before the flight and have a cup of coffee just before you land.

Diet is also a contributor. Charles Ehret developed the now-famous anti–jet lag diet, which suggests alternate days of "feasting" and "fasting." He also recommends setting your watch to the time zone of your destination to start acclimating yourself to the time change. Typically each time zone crossed requires about one day of adjustment! Every cell in the body is akin to a clock and these tiny timepieces are all brought together by a special "pacemaker" in the brain.

Naturally, it's important not to shortchange yourself on sleep before the trip or you'll only make your jet lag worse. So will alcohol.

THROWING RICE AT THE WEDDING COUPLE IS GOOD LUCK

"The bride was pregnant so everyone threw puffed rice." DICK CAVETT

The throwing of confetti or rice over the new married couple is a time-honored superstition to bestow fertility. In some countries they throw a slipper (rather painful if it hits one of them on the head).

Traditionally, confetti or rice was thrown *around* the couple—it was regarded as unlucky if it hit them. Now the tradition varies slightly. Birds eat the raw rice, which can cause illness or death. So now, according to *You and Your Wedding* by Winifred Grey, people often throw "rose petals, confetti and birdseed." It's a wedding gift for the birds as well.

RAW STEAK WILL MAKE THAT BLACK EYE GO AWAY

"Never argue with a doctor, he has inside information." BOB AND RAY

Remember the fifties? The ever-suave Rock is pursuing the su-perpure Doris. She misinterprets some innocent remark as a brazen affront and *pow!!* Cut to Rock, with a steak over his eye.

But what are the properties in steak that made the old wives go rushing to the butchers? The answer here is that it isn't the raw steak that makes the swelling go down, it's the coldness of the refrigerated meat. If you're a vegetarian, use iceberg lettuce!

Philadelphia ophthalmologist Jack Jeffers tells us that the black and blue swelling is caused by internal bleeding. When something cold makes contact, the blood vessels shrink and so does the tissue around your eye. Dr. Jeffers suggests applying an ice pack for the first twenty-four to forty-eight hours.

Consider yourself lucky that we live in such a medically enlight-ened age. In days of yore a black eye could cause the doctors to

108

run for leeches. Thank goodness people eventually looked for less distressing cures and the practice of treating the swelling with bovine flesh became widespread. "Sirloin steak is what my father used," says Jimmy, a second-generation butcher at Richard and Vinnie's Quality Meats in Brooklyn.

Getting back to more up-to-date remedies, we have learned of something called "The Tyson Treatment," presumably named for the incarcerated boxer. "Trainers use on the boxer's eye what looks like a small metal iron," explains ophthalmologist Dave Smith, who has examined hundreds of boxing-related eye injuries. "It's extremely cold, and they use it to control the immediate hemorrhage so that the swelling is minimized. You can use the same sort of treatment by getting a cold soda can and holding it against the eye intermittently (five to ten minutes every fifteen minutes) until you get some ice on it," says Dr. Smith. "Make sure the can is clean and then hold it lightly against your cheek, not your eye. Do not put any pressure on your eyeball."

If the pain is getting worse and you're thinking of taking aspirin, think again. "Aspirin is an anticoagulant, meaning the blood won't clot as well," says Dr. Jeffers. "You may wind up with a bigger bruise." Take an acetaminophen-based pain reliever (such as Tylenol) instead.

And, as if you didn't have enough to worry about, hope that you don't have a cold when you receive your sock in the eye. "Sometimes the injury can fracture the bone of your eye socket, and blowing your nose can force air out of your sinus adjacent to the socket," says Dr. Jeffers. "The air gets injected under your skin, making the eyelids swell even more."

The bottom line is that anything cold will work on a black eye—throw the steak on the grill for later.

AN OLD WIVES' AFTERWORD

So, what have we learned . . . ?

Simply this: old wives' tales are rather sweet, often naive attempts to grapple with the intractable, incomprehensible, and just plain difficult universe around us. It is a universe with few truths and fewer absolutes. Yet, we poor humans are forced to deal with it every day, to make firm decisions on the shaky foundations of ignorance, to behave as if we knew what it's all about, when obviously we don't. No wonder the old wives searched for clear and present truths. Admittedly, the truths they found were often, to put it mildly, a little off the mark. But they were motivated by the honest attempts of our foremothers to protect themselves, their families, their young.

So don't feel bad the next time you find yourself facing some brazen whippersnappers who, unwilling to accept your sage counsel, brand your warning as an "old wives' tale." You may tell them smugly that a lot of those old wives knew well and truly what they were talking about. You may omit the equally true but rather embarrassing fact that often they did not! And you may console yourself that, even if you are totally wrong (or perhaps *especially* if you are totally wrong), you are simply staking your place as part of a tradition as old as humankind itself . . . if you don't know, if you're unsure, if you can't see the truth clearly, then make up your own immutable truth and unwaveringly believe in *that*.

The old wives bid you adieu. And remember to wear a sweater when you go out tonight!